REBUILDING A POST-EXILIC COMMUNITY

Rebuilding a Post-exilic Community

The *Golah* and the "Other" in the Book of Ezra

Chingboi Guite Phaipi

Foreword by Ralph W. Klein

PICKWICK Publications · Eugene, Oregon

REBUILDING A POST-EXILIC COMMUNITY
The Golah Community and the "Other" in the Book of Ezra

Copyright © 2019 Chingboi Guite Phaipi. All rights reserved. Except for brief quotations in critical publications or reviews, no part of this book may be reproduced in any manner without prior written permission from the publisher. Write: Permissions, Wipf and Stock Publishers, 199 W. 8th Ave., Suite 3, Eugene, OR 97401.

Pickwick Publications
An Imprint of Wipf and Stock Publishers
199 W. 8th Ave., Suite 3
Eugene, OR 97401

www.wipfandstock.com

PAPERBACK ISBN: 978-1-5326-6480-9
HARDCOVER ISBN: 978-1-5326-6481-6
EBOOK ISBN: 978-1-5326-6482-3

Cataloguing-in-Publication data:

Names: Phaipi, Chingboi Guite, author. | Klein, Ralph W., foreword.
Title: Rebuilding a post-exilic community : the golah community and the "other" in the book of Ezra / Chingboi Guite Phaipi. ; foreword by Ralph W. Klein.
Description: Eugene, OR: Pickwick Publications, 2019. | Includes bibliographical references.
Identifiers: ISBN: 978-1-5326-6480-9 (paperback). | ISBN: 978-1-5326-6481-6 (hardcover). | ISBN: 978-1-5326-6482-3 (ebook).
Subjects: LCSH: Bible.—Ezra—Criticism, interpretation, etc. | Bible.—Nehemiah—Criticism, interpretation, etc. | Ethnicity—Religious aspects. | Ezra (Biblical figure). | Nehemiah—(Governor of Judah).
Classification: BS1355.52 P45 2019 (print). | BS1355.52 (epub).

Manufactured in the U.S.A.   SEPTEMBER 16, 2019

To my parents
Lianzagin Guite and Donzaching Guite

Who taught me to embrace difference with love,
Who welcome multiculturalism into their hearts and home
Who have inspired and nurtured me to be who I am today.

Contents

Foreword / Ralph W. Klein | ix

Acknowledgments | xi

Abbreviations | xiii

Introduction | 1

1. Identifications and Relationship of the *Golah* and the "Other" in the Book of Ezra | 9

2. The First Encounter of the Golah and Their Adversaries (Ezra 4:1–5) | 40

3. "Other" People Join the Passover Celebration (Ezra 6:19–22) | 60

4. Rebuilding the *Golah* Community under Ezra (Ezra 9–10) | 76

Conclusion | 106

Appendix 1: People/s of the Land/s | 113

Appendix 2: The Law of YHWH/God/Moses | 123

Bibliography | 129

Foreword

IN THE YEARS I have known Chingboi Guite she has earned a Masters degree and a PhD degree in Old Testament from McCormick Theological Seminary and the Lutheran School of Theology at Chicago, two seminaries that share a common campus. I have had her in graduate seminars and participated in her Field Examination and the defense of her dissertation. Klaus-Peter Adam, my successor at LSTC, was her advisor, but I accompanied her closely in writing and rewriting the chapters of her dissertation.

She describes herself as a timid woman from northeast India, which I would supplement with these words: who found her scholarly identity and her voice in this dissertation.

She used a synchronic literary method, investigating the final form of the book of Ezra. Whatever sources may lie behind the book of Ezra were brought together by a single author who is responsible for Ezra in its final form. The model for this type of scholarship is found in Tamara Cohn Eskenazi. Chingboi's focus is on the *golah* group, which forms the protagonists in Ezra, and they stand opposed by the "other." The *golah* group had returned from the exile in Babylon and separated themselves from the uncleanness of the nations. The "other" group comprises the adversaries of Judah and Benjamin, who had supposedly not separated themselves from the uncleanness of the nations of the land. The "other" group may have included those who were not the *golah*, were non-exiled Jews, or even in part non-Jews. But the constituent members of this group are not always clear to the modern reader.

In Ezra 4:1–5 the "other" group, despite being called adversaries of Judah and Benjamin, claimed to worship YHWH, the God of the *golah* group and offered to assist them in rebuilding the temple in Jerusalem, an offer that was refused, and the rebuilding of the temple was delayed by them until the reign of Darius.

Foreword

In Ezra 9–10 members of the *golah* were accused of marrying women from the "other" group, and the *golah* group decided that these women and their children had abominations and should be sent away, although the numbers of those involved in such marriages are surprisingly small. The *golah* saw itself as a holy seed and a remnant, but such sending away of the "other" is not repeated in either testament.

A third passage in Ezra 6:21 describes "other" Jews who had separated themselves from the uncleanness of the nations to eat the Passover with members of the *golah*. Passover was eaten by the people of Israel who had returned from exile, and also by all who had joined them and separated themselves from the pollutions of the nations of the land to worship YHWH, the God of Israel. Chingboi argues convincingly against an alternate understanding of this verse which sees those who had separated themselves from the pollutions of the nations as a periphrastic description of the *golah* group itself.

While the divisions and antagonisms in the book of Ezra have long since been resolved within Judaism, Jews, Christians, and Muslims still struggle on how they should relate themselves to the "other" or whether the "other" can somehow be included instead of being seen as different or other. Chingboi's Christian tribe, the Paite, in northeast India also faces such a challenge.

This is by no means the eschaton in interfaith relationships, but Chingboi's progress in fact is much like what Hermann Gunkel wrote in the preface to his classic commentary on the Psalter: "When I am at the end, I am only just beginning."

Whatever has happened to that timid woman from northeast India? In writing this dissertation she has found a new scholarly identity and her own voice, and in these same years she has become a mother to two lovely daughters. That's why we now joyfully call her Dr. Chingboi Guite.

Ralph W. Klein
Christ Seminary-Seminex Professor of Old Testament *emeritus*
Lutheran School of Theology at Chicago

Acknowledgments

THIS HUMBLE AND EARNEST endeavor is accomplished only through the support of so many people. I give all glory and my gratitude to God for providing me all of my needs and walking with me all along my journey to accomplish this project.

This book is a revised version of my doctoral dissertation submitted to the Lutheran School of Theology at Chicago. I am deeply grateful to Dr. Klaus-Peter Adam, my academic advisor, for all his kind and generous support. I am forever indebted to Dr. Ralph W. Klein, professor emeritus at LSTC, who graciously guided me in my dissertation, and more so for his mentorship, who with such vast knowledge and experience guided me with utmost humility and care for a timid northeast India girl like me. I am sincerely thankful to Dr. Melody Knowles, Vice President of Academic Affairs at the Virginia Theological Seminary, a renowned scholar in my area of study, for her encouragements and support of my research work. I am also very blessed to have Dr. Esther Menn, the Dean of Faculty at LSTC, who always supported me in my studies and life in LSTC.

This project would not have been accomplished without the ever present support of Rob Worley, Director of the Language Resource and Writing Center (LRWC), who is my supervisor, but also friend and mentor. I am deeply grateful for the prayers, encouragements, ministry opportunities, and friendships given to me by the Chicago Zomi Bethel Church (CZBC) and the First Baptist Church of Chicago (FBCC). LRWC friends, CZBC and FBCC communities have been my family here in Chicago, who fill the places of my parents, brothers and sisters, nieces and nephews when I am so far away from home. I would not have made it without their unending support.

Most of all, I am grateful for the support of my family: my husband Nengsuanthang Phaipi, my two beautiful little daughters, Chingnunhoih

Acknowledgments

and Lianjarzou, who stood by me and always cheered me up throughout this journey. My family back home in India: my mom and dad, brother and sisters, and all of my in-laws, for their unconditional support through prayers and encouragements on this journey. Finally, I thank Pickwick Publications of Wipf and Stock Publishers for producing my work in print.

Abbreviations

BDB	Francis Brown, S. R. Driver, and Charles A. Briggs, *Hebrew and English Lexicon of the Old Testament*. Oxford: Clarendon, 1907 (corr. ed., 1972)
Bib	*Biblica*
BibInt	*Biblical Interpretation*
BZAW	Beihefte zur Zeitschrift für die alttestamentliche Wissenschaft
COS	*The Context of Scripture*. Edited by William W. Hallo. 4 vols. Leiden: Brill, 1997–2017
HUCA	*Hebrew Union College Annual*
JAOS	*Journal of the American Oriental Society*
JBL	*Journal of Biblical Literature*
JBQ	*Jewish Bible Quarterly*
JHS	*Journal of Hebrew Scriptures*
JNSL	*Journal of Northwest Semitic Languages*
JSJ	*Journal for the Study of Judaism in the Persian, Hellenistic and Roman Periods*
JSOT	*Journal for the Study of the Old Testament*
JSOTSup	Journal for the Study of the Old Testament Supplements
JTS	*Journal of Theological Studies*
LHBOTS	Library of Hebrew Bible/Old Testament Studies
MT	Masoretic Text

Abbreviations

OTL	Old Testament Library
TDOT	*Theological Dictionary of the Old Testament.* 16 vols. Edited by G. Johannes Botterweck, Helmer Ringgren, and Heinz-Josef Fabray. Grand Rapids: Eerdmans, 1974–2018
VT	*Vetus Testamentum*
ZAW	*Zeitschrift für die alttestamentliche Wissenschaft*

Introduction

"Other" people are the cause of dread, and they are adversarial, and they are to be sent away from our community. Such could be the impression that one gets from different parts of the book of Ezra (Ezra 3:3; 4:1; 10:3, respectively). At the same time, there is another part where "other" people are welcome to join the community (Ezra 6:21). The book of Ezra, then, seems to have an inconsistent attitude towards the "other"—from dread to adversarial, from welcoming to sending them away. In the narrative, as the returning exiles rebuild the temple and the community, who constitute the protagonist and who constitute the "other"? Is the apparently inconsistent attitude of the *golah* community towards the "other" arbitrary or does it evolve from a coherent basis? In order to answer these questions, the whole narrative has to be read.

From a literary analysis of the book of Ezra, I will make two arguments. First, the narrative is primarily about the *golah* community. The "other" group receives at best vague identities, and mentioned mostly with respect to the *golah* group, whether positively or negatively. As such, the "other" group is a broad group that comprises any and all non-*golah* people. Secondly, there is a coherent basis behind the *golah*'s inconsistent attitudes towards the "other" people. That coherent basis is that the *golah* community's self-perception of being the "holy seed" and the spared "remnant" compels them to keep themselves apart from "other" people. The expectation that they keep themselves apart is present throughout the narrative, which is sometimes expressed implicitly in their fulfillment of it (Ezra 3–4) and at other times spelled out directly in their failure to maintain it (Ezra 9–10). That same basis is also what allows them to welcome "other" people among them in the Passover account (Ezra 6:19–21).

I will use "*golah* community" for the protagonists of the book of Ezra as it is the key term used in the text. The term *golah* (*gôlâ*) can refer to different things—the condition of being deported from one's homeland, the place where one is deported, or the deportees themselves collectively.[1] In the book of Ezra, it is used mainly in reference to those exiles who returned from Babylon to Judah, and rebuilding the temple and their community. Even though it is not the only term used to identify the protagonist group, this term best sums up their identity as mostly made up of those who returned from the Babylonian exile.[2] The term *golah* appears eleven times in the book of Ezra, and in most cases refers to the collection of people, once as the state of being in exile ("captivity" [Ezra 2:1]). While some translate it as "returnees" or "returned exiles," the text does not explicitly state that it is exclusively formed of only those who returned. Thus, although predominantly formed of those who returned, the text appears to leave some openness.

Methodology

This study will consider the book of Ezra, without the book of Nehemiah. While there are general negative attitudes towards the "other" in both Ezra and Nehemiah, they clearly have different concerns. For instance, for Nehemiah, Sabbath, language, or political issues are the mentioned concerns (Neh 13:16, 24, 26), which are not the highlighted concerns in Ezra. Furthermore, although traditionally Ezra and Nehemiah are taken to be a single work (Ezra–Nehemiah), the debate over the dependency or independency of these works remains unresolved. Thus, while there are similarities and possible connections between Ezra and Nehemiah (as well as with Chronicles) at some level, Ezra can still be seen as an independent work from Nehemiah or Chronicles.[3]

---

1. In texts from exilic and post-exilic periods, the term *golah* is mostly used in the sense of the deportees (the people) (Jer 28:4; 29:1, 20, 31; Ezek 1:1; 3:11, 15; Zech 6:10; Ezra 1:11; 9:4; 10:6). See Blenkinsopp, *Judaism*, 78–79.

2. The main terms used to identify the members of this community are the *golah* and Israel: the *golah* (Ezra 2:1; 8:35; 9:4; 10:6), sons of the *golah* (4:1; 6:16, 19, 20; 10:7, 16), Israel (2:2b; 3:1; 6:16, 17, 21; 7:7, 13; 8:25; 9:1, 4; 10:5, 10), or "Jews" in the Aramaic section (4:23; 5:1; 6:8, 14). Other terms include: all those who came from the captivity (3:8), those who came up from the captivity (2:1), Judah and Benjamin (1:5; 4:1; 10:9), remnant (9:8, 13, 14, 15). For the antagonist, non-*golah* people in general, "other/s" will be used to encompass the different terms used in the text, such as peoples of the lands (3:3; 9:1, 2, 11), peoples of the land (10:2, 11), people of the land (4:4), nations of the land (6:21), adversaries (4:1), foreign (10:2, 10).

3. I agree with scholars who view it as an independent work, such as H. G. M

Introduction

This study will be based on a literary synchronic approach to the final form with focus on how the characters and their relationships are portrayed.[4] Structurally, two main sections can be identified in the book of Ezra: the rebuilding of the Temple (Ezra 1–6) and Ezra Memoir (Ezra 7–10; Neh 8:1–9:3). In regards to style and genre, both prose narrative and official documents are found in both sections. There are changes in the language and literary style and genre, too. For instance, within Ezra 1–6, there is a section in Aramaic (4:8–6:18), and within Ezra 7–10, there is also an Aramaic section (7:12–26). In addition, the text also presents some discrepancies in historical chronology as the chronology in the text does not match extrabiblical chronology.[5] Despite these discrepancies, it can be observed that a coherent theme runs throughout the narrative, as will be detailed later.

In terms of authorship and composition, as Williamson argues, it is probable that a single author is responsible for putting together the sections from various existing documents and materials—such as the Edict of Cyrus (Ezra 1:2–4), an inventory of temple vessels (Ezra 1:9–11), a list of returnees (Ezra 2), letters (Ezra 4:6–6:22), the accounts of Ezra and Nehemiah (Ezra 7–Neh 13), with added narratives (Ezra 3:1–4:5) to form the final form.[6] It is also quite possible, as Japhet argues, for that author to produce the book "all at once."[7] There is no reason to doubt that a single

---

Williamson, Sara Japhet, and Bob Becking. See Becking, *Ezra, Nehemiah*, 5.

4. This approach is not to disregard the complexity of sources or compositional stages the book of Ezra might have been through. Indeed, it is easy to identify possible different types of sources in the text of Ezra. For instance, one type of source would be the documents, which would have been available in some form to the author/compiler: the Edict of Cyrus (Ezra 1:2–4), the list of temple vessels (Ezra 1:9–11), the list of returnees (Ezra 2), the letters (Ezra 4:6–7, 8–16, 17–22; 5:6–17; 6:3–12), and the Ezra Memoir (Ezra 7–10). And another type of source would be the narratives, which would be penned by the author, and could possibly have undergone more than one composition or redaction process. See Williamson, *Ezra, Nehemiah*, xxiv; Blenkinsopp, *Ezra-Nehemiah*, 42.

5. Japhet discusses in detail the problems within these sections as well as chronological discrepancies. See Japhet, *From the Rivers of Babylon*, 246–51, 254–60.

6. Williamson, "Composition of Ezra i–vi."

7. Japhet, *From the Rivers of Babylon*, 245–67. It may be noted that there are others who view that the composition would have taken in different stages. For instance, Williamson views that the Ezra Memoir (Ezra 7–10; Neh 8) was combined with the Nehemiah Memoir (Neh 1–7; 12:27–43; 13:4–31), to which most of the rest of the Nehemiah material was added. Then, Ezra 1–6 was added, as the introduction. See Williamson, *Ezra, Nehemiah*, xxxiv. Blenkinsopp views that Ezra 1–6 was composed first, to which its following materials were added—the Ezra Memoir, the Nehemiah Memoir, and then

author could produce the narratives and carefully put them together with the other available documents into the current form. As will be seen in the analysis, a coherent theme runs through the whole book of Ezra, which implies a single author responsible for the whole book in its final form. This author might be working near to the events described, perhaps around 400 BCE.[8] For the purpose of this study, no further discussion on the nature of composition, authorship or dating is necessary as the finished form will be studied.

I follow Eskenazi's literary methodology in her book, *In An Age of Prose: A Literary Approach to Ezra-Nehemiah*, which is indeed a pioneer and groundbreaking shift for the Ezra–Nehemiah studies for a literary approach on the final form. As Eskenazi rightly challenges, the history of interpretation of Ezra, mostly concentrated in other methodologies such as source criticism or historical criticism, still leaves the complexities unresolved.[9] In a sense, Eskenazi was taking up on Childs's canonical approach. Childs finds that the traditional historical critical trends in the studies of Ezra–Nehemiah, which mostly start with the formation or composition of the book, result in unfruitful interpretation of the text. As such, he proposes that the text in its canonical shape can truly convey its message without completely solving the historical, source or literary problems.[10] As I employ literary approach with a focused interest on the portrayal of the protagonist *golah* group and antagonist "other" group/s in the book of Ezra I differ from Eskenazi's study which covers the general theme that runs throughout Ezra and Nehemiah. It is my contention that from studying the whole narrative of the book of Ezra, one will be able to evaluate the seemingly inconsistent

---

the rest of Nehemiah. See Blenkinsopp, *Ezra–Nehemiah*, 41–47. In yet another model, Pakkala argues for several editors working in several stages—the *golah editors*, who were concerned with boundaries, combined Ezra 1–6 and Ezra 7–10 (including Neh 8) and made the exilic community the central actors. Then the Priestly and Levitical editors, who came much later, edited the material with their own concerns about their positions in the community. See Pakkala, "Exile and the Exiles," 98–99. Despite these difficulties, it can be observed that a coherent theme runs through the whole narrative, and as such, I agree with Japhet's argument that the author could certainly have compiled "all at once" following a clear theme.

8. Ezra and his team are the second group of returnees in the book of Ezra. If they returned during the reign of Artaxerxes (Ezra 7:1), assuming it to be Artaxerxes I, it would be during 465–525 BCE. See Williamson, *Ezra, Nehemiah*, xxxv–xxxvi.

9. Eskenazi, *In an Age of Prose*, 184.

10. Childs, *Introduction to the Old Testament*, 628–38.

INTRODUCTION

attitude towards the "other" and investigate if there is a consistent reason behind such inconsistencies.

Sections

Chapter 1 is an overall survey of the whole book of Ezra with focus on the identifications and characterizations of the protagonist *golah* group and "other" people. What becomes apparent is that the narrative is primarily about the *golah* group, and is less interested in the "other" people, who are often mentioned only for the sake of the *golah* group, positively or negatively. With no specifications, any and all non-*golah* people are treated together in one broad group of "other" people.

Chapter 2 is an analysis of the first accounted interaction of the *golah* group and "other" people, designated as "adversaries of Judah and Benjamin" and "people of the land" (Ezra 4:1–5). Claiming to worship the God of the *golah* community, the "adversaries" proposed to join in rebuilding the temple, but the *golah* group denied them, so they thwarted the work of the *golah* group. Cultic difference between the two groups is evident from their exchange of conversation, which would be the drive behind the *golah* group to remain apart from the "other" people.

Chapter 3 analyzes the only account of an admission of "other" people into the *golah* community. "Other" people who had separated themselves from the uncleanness of the nations of the land were welcomed to join the *golah* group in the Passover to worship YHWH (Ezra 6:19–21). Clearly, they are not random "other" people but those who had met the prerequisite of the *golah* community. In welcoming "other" people, then, the *golah* community still maintained the same criterion as in their keeping apart from "other" people.

Chapter 4 is an analysis of the most hostile attitude towards the "other." Having come to the realization that they have committed an unfaithfulness by failing to remain apart from "other" people and even marrying their women, the *golah* community resolved to send away their foreign wives and children (Ezra 9–10). Harsh as the resolution may seem, the strong self-perception of the *golah* community—as the "holy seed" and "remnant" and the resulting expectation to remain apart from "other" people required that they take this path.

Finally, in the conclusion, after noting the findings from the literary analysis of the book of Ezra, two brief remarks will be made. First, I will discuss how the varying degrees of the attitude of the *golah* community can be understood by following the timeline of the community as they were returning and settling back in the land. Second, I will reflect, *albeit* very briefly, on how the *golah* community's situation might resonate in some way with my tribe, the Paite (Zomi), today.

We now turn to the complete survey of the narrative to establish the larger theme, followed by a detail analysis of how the larger theme plays out in individual accounts. For reference, an outline of the book of Ezra is included below.

Outline of the Book of Ezra (including Neh 8)

I. Permission and Return to Jerusalem (Ezra 1–2)
    (i) 1:1 Introduction
    (ii) 1:2–4 Edict of Cyrus
    (iii) 1:5–8 Preparation for return
    (iv) 1:9–11 List of vessels brought back to Jerusalem
    (v) 2:1–70 List of people who returned to Jerusalem
        2:2–35 lay people
        2:36–40 the priests and Levites
        2:41 the singers
        2:42 the gatekeepers
        2:43–58 the temple servants
        2:59–63 those who could not confirm their genealogy
        2:64–69 total number of people, record of the offerings
    (vi) 2:70 Conclusion

II. Back in the Land, Working on the Building Project (Ezra 3:1—6:15)
    (i) 3:1–6 Precursory work: the altar
    (ii) 3:7–13 Laying of the temple foundation
    (iii) 4:1–24 Encountering difficulties in building project
        4:1–5 "adversaries of Judah and Benjamin"
        4:6 an accusation letter during reign of Ahasuerus (Xerxes)
        4:7–16 two accusations during reign of Artaxerxes
        4:17–24 king's reply to accusation/s; cessation of building work

Introduction

    (iv) 5:1–2 Building work resumed after prophesies of Haggai and Zechariah
    (v) 5:3–5 Being questioned by Tattenai and reported to king Darius
    (vi) 5:6–17 The letter from Tattenai to king Darius
    (vii) 6:1–2 King Darius's command and finding of Cyrus's edict
    (viii) 6:3–5 Copy of Cyrus's edict
    (ix) 6:6–12 Darius's letter of support for the building project
    (x) 6:13–22 Dedication of the temple, Passover celebration

III. More Return Under the Leadership Of Ezra (Ezra 7–8)
    (i) 7:1–6 Introduction of Ezra the person
    (ii) 7:7–10 Summary of the journey
    (iii) 7:11–26 Commissioning letter of Artaxerxes to Ezra
    (iv) 7:27–28 Ezra's praise (doxology)
    (v) 8:1–20 List of those who returned with Ezra
    (vi) 8:21–36 Ezra's account of leading people back to Jerusalem

IV. Ezra Led the Community (Neh 8; Ezra 9–10)
    (i) Neh 8:1–12 Reading of the Law
    (ii) Neh 8:13–18 Festival of Sukkoth
    (iii) Ezra 9:1–2 Report of Unfaithfulness
    (iv) Ezra 9:3–15 Reaction from Ezra
    (v) Ezra 10:1–17 People's Response
    (vi) Ezra 10:18–43 List of men who married foreign women
    (vii) Ezra 10:44 Conclusion

1

Identifications and Relationship of the *Golah* and the "Other" in the Book of Ezra

THIS CHAPTER IS A survey of the book of Ezra, identifying the terms and descriptions used for the protagonist group, the *golah*, as well as for the "other." The protagonist group—the *golah*—is primarily the group that had been in exile in Babylon and who are then allowed to return to Jerusalem by the Persian king Cyrus. The different terms and descriptions that are employed for the *golah* group and for the "other" group/s throughout the Ezra narrative will be identified, and the contexts in which they are used will be studied. This survey will help to evaluate whether the attitude of the *golah* towards "other/s" and the relationship between the *golah* and "other/s" throughout the book are coherent or varying, as well as what the factors that determine such attitude/s and relationship/s are.

The survey of the narrative will reveal that the narrative is primarily about the *golah* community and that one of their core self-conceptions is that they are set apart by and for YHWH. As such, they are to keep themselves apart from "other" people, unless the "other" people have also separated themselves from the things unacceptable to YHWH and thus for the *golah* community. The narrative sets out with the protagonist group, the *golah*, being granted a return to their land by an "other," Cyrus, the king of Persia.

Rebuilding a Post-exilic Community

Ezra 1–2: Permission and Preparation to Return to Jerusalem

At the outset of the book of Ezra, the *golah* are granted permission by Cyrus, the king of Persia, to go back to Jerusalem and rebuild the house of YHWH.

> Who among you from all his people—may his God be with him, and let him go up to Jerusalem which is in Judah, and let him build the house of YHWH, the God of Israel, he is the God who is in Jerusalem. (Ezra 1:3)[1]

In this verse the definitive term for the protagonist group is "his people," that is, "YHWH's people." Those YHWH's people in exile are now granted permission to return to Jerusalem to build the house of God. This raises the question if the imperial command for rebuilding the temple is exclusively for these YHWH's people who return from Babylonian exile to Jerusalem, and, subsequently, whether or not any Israelite/Jew who had not been exiled and stayed in Judea is considered to be among YHWH's people. These questions cannot be answered merely from this immediate context and will be engaged as we encounter similar attributions throughout the narrative. Yet, what is observable here is that from the outset of the narrative, important aspects of the *golah* community are seen—that the *golah* group is YHWH's people, exiled and authorized to build the house of God in Jerusalem.

The following verse tells that while not everyone went back, those who remain were also expected to help those who returned with silver and gold and goods and animals, as well as freewill offerings (Ezra 1:4). That is, all who had been in the exile were expected or encouraged to participate in the temple building project. The next verse further describes those who went back.

> The heads of the families of Judah and Benjamin, and the priests and Levites, arose, as well as all whose spirit God stirred, to go to build the house of YHWH which is in Jerusalem. (Ezra 1:5)

The heads of the families (literally, "heads of the fathers")[2] of Judah and Benjamin, the priests and Levites, and "those whose spirits were stirred

---

1. This and all other biblical quotations are my own translations.
2. In the post-exilic period, the title "heads of the families" stands for the larger, extended family, not just the immediate family (Williamson, *Ezra, Nehemiah*, 15). This "extended family" group was a regular sociological division of people in the Persian

Identifications & Relationship of the *Golah* & the "Other"

by YHWH" prepared to go to Jerusalem in response to the permission from Cyrus. That is, lay leaders, cultic leaders and some lay people described by "all whose spirits God stirred" were preparing to return in response to the decree of king Cyrus. This statement implies that those lay members of the *golah* who return were not random people but those people who were actually stirred by YHWH to return to Jerusalem and fulfill the task of rebuilding the house of God there. The notion of YHWH stirring up the spirit is already seen in Ezra 1:1, where the spirit of Cyrus is stirred by YHWH, resulting in the proclamation of permission for the exiles to return to Jerusalem to build the temple.[3] Thus, YHWH is the real source of inspiration and actions—for Cyrus to allow the return and for those who actually returned. YHWH is central in the life of the *golah* community.

In Ezra 2, we have a more detailed list of the people who return from the Babylonian exile to Jerusalem.

> These are the people of the province who returned from the captivity of the exile whom Nebuchadnezzar king of Babylon had taken (into) exile to Babylon. They returned to Jerusalem and Judah, each to his town. (Ezra 2:1)

In this verse, the phrases employed—"people of the province"[4] and "those who returned from the captivity of the exile whom Nebuchadnezzar had taken into exile"—imply once again that being in exile, and then returning, is one of the main defining criteria for the *golah* group. It implies that the list more or less now represents the *golah* community who are now in the province Judah.[5] The list categorizes the *golah* community into Israel (lay people) (Ezra 2:2b–35), Priests (2:36–39), and Levites (2:40–42).[6] The

---

period; a grouping between the larger tribe and the smaller family grouping. As such, the "fathers" in this verse would be more like "clans" (*mišpāḥâ*) of pre-exilic times. See Klein, *Ezra & Nehemiah*, 679.

3. The term for stirring (*'ûr*) points to being stirred or roused to activity (Judg 5:12). In the *Hiphil*, it is mostly YHWH who is the cause of the act of stirring/arousing and thus of the activity (Isa 41:2, 25; 45:13; Hag 1:14).

4. The "province" here can be either referring to Judah where the returnees now live or Babylon from where they came. It seems more plausible that this province is referring to a province in Judah, where the *golah* are settling. The author of Ezra in general does not seem to be so interested in providing details of Babylon or how life was there, at least not explicitly.

5. Klein, *Ezra & Nehemiah*, 685.

6. It is common in Ezra that the *golah* group is listed into priests, Levites, and laity (Ezra 2:2b, 36, 40; 3:12; 6:16; 7:7; 9:1).

list continues with names of singers, gatekeepers, and temple servants (Ezra 2:43–58), revealing the purpose of the *golah* community to be rebuilding the temple and making it function again.

If the list is to provide the decisive factors or criteria for the *golah* community, it is still not without problems. Noteworthy is the difference in the manner of identification where some are identified by father's names (Ezra 2:2b–19) and others by domicile (Ezra 2:20–35).[7] While the reason behind the recording of some people by their towns and others by their father's names is not stated, all those included in the list could be safely considered to be part of the *golah* community.

As Williamson argues, those identified by father's names could be those who had recently returned from the exile, and those identified by their domicile those "who had stayed in the land but who still felt themselves sufficiently related by ties of blood, social orientation, and religion to join and be accepted by those returning to rebuild the temple."[8] Listing by father's names could also be a way to claim heredity, and listing by place names could be a way to claim the land as these places are around Jerusalem—Gibbar, Bethlehem, Netophah, Kiriath-Arim, Michmas, Nebo, Machbis, Elam, Harim, Lod, Hadid, Ono, and many originally belonged to Benjamin (Ezra 2:20–35).[9] At any rate, the community that is being formed might not be made exclusively of those who returned from exile. In the next section also (Ezra 2:59–63), some people in the list face the problem of legitimacy so they could not confirm their Israelite status.

> And these are the ones who came from Tel Methal, Tel Harsha, Cherub, Addan, Immer. They were not able to tell if their fathers' family and their descendants were from Israel. Among the

---

7. This switching from one form of identification to another without a stated reason may be an indication of the composite nature of the list. It is not my interest to analyze the compositional stages or sources of the list but rather to examine what the current list conveys about the *golah* community. For a discussion on the composite nature of the list in chapter 2, see Williamson, *Ezra, Nehemiah*, 28–32.

8. Williamson also asserts that it is not uncommon in the early Persian period to use both genealogy and geography for identification (Williamson, "Family in Persian Period Judah," 479).

9. The towns in this passage are believed to be proximate to Jerusalem (Redditt, *Ezra-Nehemiah*, 82). Many of these towns seem to belong originally to Benjamin (such as Anathoth, Azmaveth, Ramah and Geba, Bethel and Ai, Jericho) (Blenkinsopp, *Ezra-Nehemiah*, 86–87). These places thus link with the naming of "Judah and Benjamin" for the *golah* community in Ezra (Ezra 1:5; 4:1).

> descendants of Deliyah, the descendants of Tobiah, the descendants of Nekoda: six hundred and fifty two.
>
> Among the descendants of the priests: the descendants of Habiyyah, the descendants of Hakkoz, the descendants of Barzillai who took a wife from the daughters of Barzillai the Gilead, and was called by their name. These sought their record from among those enrolled by genealogy but they were not found. So, they were excluded from priesthood as polluted. The governor said to them that they should not eat from the holy of the holies until a priest with Urim and Thummim decides. (Ezra 2:59–63)

This passage lists lay people and priests who could not confirm their heredity as Israelite. The lay people are recorded with domiciles. The first two place names—Tel Methal, Tel Harsha—seem to be Babylonian, and the later three place names—Cherub, Addan, Immer—are unidentified. This suggests that the exiled Jews were also settled in some places in Babylon which were unoccupied.[10] It could be that these people lost their genealogical records in the exile (in the journey to Babylon, while in Babylon, or on their return to Jerusalem). As such, the best information they have is their place of settlement in Babylon. Seemingly, if they were able to present their ancestors' name as Israelite or at least their domicile to be in Judah (or Benjamin), they would not have been put in detention (cf. Ezra 2:20–35, where no problem is attached with those from Judah and Benjamin). In other words, if these people were from Judah, they might not have to face the question of genealogical correctness. As such, being in exile and returning to Judah alone does not grant an immediate entry into the *golah* community.

After those listed by domiciles, three other families—of Delaiah, of Tobiah, of Nekoda—are also listed as not able to confirm if their fathers and their descendants were Israelites. Since their names are Yahwistic it is questionable that they would be proselytes.[11] No conclusive identification is possible. Finally, three groups of priests—of Habaiah, of Hakkoz, of Barzillai—also could not find their genealogical records and had to be suspended from priesthood, at least until there is a priest with Urim and Thurim (Ezra 2:61–63).[12] While the name Habaiah is unattested elsewhere

---

10. Blenkinsopp, *Ezra–Nehemiah*, 91–92; Clines, *Ezra, Nehemiah, Esther*, 58.
11. Williamson, *Ezra, Nehemiah*, 37.
12. The term "Urim and Thummim" is mentioned explicitly seven times in the Hebrew Bible (Exod 28:30; Lev 8:8; Deut 33:8; without "thummim" in Num 27:21; 1 Sam

the family of Hakkoz seems to be re-instated later (Neh 3:4). The family of Barzillai could possibly be traced back to references about king David's time—Barzillai was a wealthy Gileadite who had given shelter to David when he ran away from Absolom, and later David asked king Solomon to protect Barzillai's family (2 Sam 17:27–29; 19:31–39; 1 Kgs 2:7). Thus it is possible that Gileadites were considered to be part of Israel because of the kindness of their ancestor toward king David. At any rate, the pertinent question is whether being suspended from priesthood also puts them out of the *golah* community. They could have lost their priestly function while still remaining part of the community. It appears that unless proven wrong they are included in the list and thereby in the *golah* community. With no other "corrected list" available and no statement that they are banned from the community—the only statement being they could not confirm their Israelite geneology—these people could be said to be included as valid members. At best, it can be said that this passage presents genealogy as vital, but not as the exclusive determining factor for *golah* membership.

On the purpose of the list in Ezra 2, there are different views, such as a proof of true Israelite community with legitimate descent, a Persian tax list, or a list for claiming land rights.[13] The text, however, does not provide a special purpose, except stating it as a list of those who returned from the exile (Ezra 2:1). Thus, from a literary point of view, the list primarily serves as a record of who is (and can be) in the *golah* community,[14] though it would also provide answers if questioned by any external factor—for instance, when Tattenai asked who those involved in building the temple were (Ezra 5:4). The list reveals both exile and Israelite genealogy as primary yet not the exclusive criteria to be included in the *golah* community, since those identified by domiciles are also included. The list highlights the

---

28:6; Ezra 2:63; Neh 7:65). It is not known for sure how Urim and Thummim worked or if they were used by high priests in the second temple period. There are several theories about what they might have been or how they might have been used, such as tangible objects in boxes, single object or two objects, or possibly an alternative expression for the breastplate stones themselves, serving as lots or oracular device, as giving Yes or No answers, or as able to give more detailed answers than that. It probably was carried by the high priest, and thus would refer to the time of the reconstitution of the cultic life of the community, at which time a high priest would be there with the proper authority to decide such disputable situations. For more discussions on Urim and Thummim, see Williamson, *Ezra, Nehemiah*, 37; Houtman, "Urim and Thummim"; Bakon, "Mystery of the Urim ve-Thummim"; Fried, "Did Second Temple High Priests Possess."

13. Clines, *Ezra, Nehemiah, Esther*, 44.
14. Galling, "'Gōlā-List,'" 153, 157.

continuity with pre-exilic Israel by trying to trace their genealogy to who had been exiled to Babylon, and then returned back in the land (Ezra 2:70). This claim of being the continuity of pre-exilic Israel, will be seen repeated in the rest of the narrative.

Summary on Permission, Preparation, and Return (Ezra 1–2)

The first two chapters of Ezra are about the permission, preparation and return from the Babylonian exile to Jerusalem. Cyrus, the king of Persia, being stirred by YHWH issues an edict permitting YHWH's people to return to Jerusalem to rebuild the temple (Ezra 1:1–4). The main identifiers used for the *golah* group are YHWH's people (Ezra 1:3), Judah and Benjamin (1:3), those stirred by YHWH (1:3), people of the province (2:1), those who return from the Babylonian exile (2:1), and people of Israel (2:2). The "other" in these two chapters, Cyrus the Persian king, is portrayed positively. He follows YHWH's command (Ezra 1:1–2) and lets the *golah* group return to their land (Ezra 1:3–4). Thus, the first observable point is that the narrative works primarily for the *golah* community and the "other," Cyrus, also works in support of the *golah*.

Important characteristics of the *golah* community in the beginning of the narrative (Ezra 1–2) can be listed as follows. First, being identified by "YHWH's people" "stirred by YHWH" to return and rebuild the house of the God of Israel in Jerusalem (Ezra 1:3, 5), the *golah* community and the purpose of their return are clearly seen as cultic.[15] It may also mean that the *golah* community forms the exclusive people of YHWH and is exclusively responsible for rebuilding the house of God, thereby the *golah* community is mainly presented in the narrative as a cultic community. The lay people are also addressed as "people of Israel" (Ezra 2:2), which can connote that "Israel" is reserved for those who are part of the *golah* community. At this point of the narrative, however, no firm conclusions can be drawn. Secondly, being in the Babylonian exile and then returning to Jerusalem (Ezra 2:1) as well as Israelite genealogy are vital, as seen in the list in Ezra 2. Thus, to this point of the narrative it is observable that the narrative is primarily about the *golah* community who are YHWH's people, exiled and returned to Judah, and who also have a legitimate Israelite heredity. There is no negative portrayal of the "other" in this section; rather, the only "other" in this

---

15. Knowles, *Centrality Practiced*, 86.

section, Cyrus, is supportive of the cause of the *golah* group. In the next section, however, an unfriendly attitude appears towards the "other."

Ezra 3: Back in the Land, Laying the Temple Foundation

From Ezra 3 onward, the narrative focuses on the *golah* community back in the land. In the section Ezra 3:1–4:5, we see the first encounter of the *golah* group with the "other" people as they were settling back into the land and beginning to work on the building project. The *golah* community continues to be identified as "Israelites" (literally "sons of Israel"). The *golah* group's desire to be the continuation of preexilic Israel and to perform cult correctly can be seen in their building the altar of the God of Israel "according to the law of Moses"[16] and on its foundation, that is, on its original site (Ezra 3:2–3). Also, they celebrated the festival of the Tabernacles "as is written" and performed the burnt offerings "as is prescribed" (Ezra 3:4). The installation of the altar also reveals the centrality of the cult in the life of the *golah* community—it was the first thing the *golah* did when they arrived and settled, even before beginning the temple itself. After all, the purpose of the *golah* group's return was to rebuild the house of YHWH, that is, to re-establish the temple for the worship of YHWH, thus building the altar seems a legitimate first step in working out their temple building project.

Ezra 3:3 mentions the relationship of the *golah* with the "other" group, albeit without a physical encounter: "They set up the altar upon its foundations, although[17] dread was upon them from the peoples of the lands. And they offered burnt offerings to YHWH in the morning and in the evening." This verse is the first instance in the narrative when the attitude of the *golah* community towards the "other," identified as "peoples of the lands," is expressed. There is no further information to identify the phrase peoples of

16. The law of Moses here is to be understood broadly as the Pentateuch.

17. I translate the Hebrew word *kî* as adversative here since it seems that the fear of the peoples of the lands was not the sole driving force for the building of the altar. I follow Fensham's translation ("in spite of") (Fensham, *Ezra and Nehemiah*, 59). There are also a few English Bible translations that use the adversative sense, such as the New Living Translation Bible ("even though"), the New King James Bible ("though"), the New Jerusalem Bible ("despite"). Other passages where *kî* has an adversative sense: Gen 31:37; Exod 13:17; 34:9; Deut 18:14; 32:52; Josh 5:5; 2 Chr 24:24; Eccl 8:6; Jer 14:12; 49:16; Lam 3:32). The alternative way to translate it is as causal—that is, they build the altar "for" or "because" they fear the peoples of the lands. In this sense of translation, they build the altar so that they can take refuge in YHWH from their fear of the people (see 1 Chr 21:28–22:1; Blenkinsopp, *Ezra-Nehemiah*, 97).

the lands.[18] The text only states that the *golah* group is afraid of these peoples of the lands. From the context, it seems that the peoples of the lands whom the *golah* group feared could be any or all of those non-*golah* people—non-exiled Jews or non-Jews, who were dwelling in the land when the *golah* group arrived. The phrase as used in the text seems to refer to those who are not worshipping YHWH, or at least in the way of the *golah* group. As will be seen repeatedly, "other" people tend to be mentioned vaguely, without further information for identification, and all non-*golah* people seem to be put together into a broad "other" people. The text is primarily interested in the *golah* group but not the "other." The text states that *golah* community built the altar even though they were in dread of the peoples of the lands.

The term for dread, *ēmâ*, carries the connotation that when someone has a dread over another, the person feels danger, insecurity or even threat.[19] Ezra 3:3 states that the altar was built "in its original site," and after the altar was built, the Tabernacles was observed "as is written" and burnt offerings were made "as is prescribed" (Ezra 3:4). It could be that an altar existed in this place during the exile, but when the *golah* returned, they saw it as incorrectly built, not following Moses's instructions, so they felt the need to build a new, correct one.[20] If the *golah* group was building a new altar to replace the one that existed, it can only be expected that they would fear that peoples of the lands would be angry.[21] It could also be that the *golah* people, who would not have been able to offer burnt offerings on an altar in the exile, were trying to carry out sacrifices as they remembered (or as they were taught, for those born in Babylon) how they were done

---

18. The phrase *people of the land* (singular) appears in Ezra 4:4, and in two plural forms—*peoples of the land* (Ezra 10:2, 11) and *peoples of the lands* (Ezra 3:3; 9:1–2, 11). See Appendix for more discussion.

19. The term for fear (*'ēmâ*) is used in some instances to indicate fear or awe of YHWH's power (Exod 15:16; 23:27; Ps 88:16; Deut 32:25; Job 9:34; 13:21). In other instances, the term connotes terror, dread or insecurity, from death or other human beings. In Gen 15:12, darkness and dread or confusion fell on Abram; in Ps 55:5, the psalter talks of terrors of death; Prov 20:2 refers to dread of a king; Job 33:7 refers to fear of human (Elihu to Job); in Job 20:25, terror comes to the wicked or godless; in Josh 2:9, the Canaanites are afraid of the spies sent by Joshua; and terror in Isa 33:18 apparently is about terror under the oppression of enemy.

20. Comparing with Jer 41:5. Many scholars hold this view—for example, Fensham, *Ezra and Nehemiah*, 59; Blenkinsopp, *Ezra-Nehemiah*, 97; Williamson, *Ezra, Nehemiah*, 46.

21. Fensham, *Ezra and Nehemiah*, 59.

"according to the law of Moses."[22] Thus, how the *golah* are now carrying out these cultic activities might be different from how the existing inhabitants did, and could also imply rejection of the existing inhabitants' ways, which would naturally invoke conflicts.

In addition, Ezra 2:70 states that those who returned from the exile dwelled in the towns, and even though it is not expressed explicitly, it can be assumed that they might have had some struggles. The *golah* returnees could have struggled to fit back on the land, trying to find homes and lands, while those who had been dwelling there might not have been so willing to give up their homes and lands to the new arrivals. There would also be tensions between the newly arrived *golah* people and those who lived there, which could cause dread on the newly returned *golah* group. What the text does reveal is that the relationship between the *golah* community and the people of the land is not amicable.

After building the altar, the *golah* community began to offer burnt offerings regularly (Ezra 3:1–6). Then, they began to lay the temple foundation (Ezra 3:7–13). Ezra 3:7 presents the *golah* group, here identified as "all those who returned from the captivity," as very careful to carry out things carefully, "according to the permission given to them by Cyrus, king of Persia" (Ezra 3:7b; cf. 4:3). This verse also portrays "others" as supportive of their project, such as the Sidonians and Tyrians bringing cedarwood from Lebanon for the temple building.[23] And thus the work on the temple began.

> And in the second year of their coming to the house of God in Jerusalem, on the second month, Zerubbabel son of Shealtiel and Jeshua son of Jozadak, and the rest of their brothers, the priests, the Levites, and all those who came back from the captivity to Jerusalem began and appointed Levites from those twenty years old and older to oversee the work of the house of YHWH. (Ezra 3:8)

This verse states that the work of the building project was being undertaken exclusively by "all those who came back from the captivity to Jerusalem," that is, the *golah* group. There is no mention if non-exiled Jews

---

22. From a later verse (Ezra 3:12), we can know that among the *golah* returnees there are some who lived in Judah and were physically exiled to Babylon, and there would also be some who were born in the exile in Babylon, and see the land (Judah/Yehud) for the first time. Some instructions to build "according to the law of Moses" are noted in Exod 20:25; Deut 27:6.

23. Eskenazi divides the "Other" in Ezra–Nehemiah into two groups—as foe and as friend, and the Sidonians and Tyrians would be among the "other" as friends. See Eskenazi, "Imagining the Other," 240.

would have participated. The emphasis on "all" who came back from the captivity then highlights the whole community's participation while also implying that they exclusively did the work of the house of YHWH. After the foundation of the temple was laid, there were celebrations with music, singing psalms and shouts and weeping (Ezra 3:10–12). The older priests, Levites and heads of the families who had seen the first temple wept at the foundation that was just laid for the new temple (whether out of joy or in disappoinment is not stated). The mention of the reaction of those who had seen the first temple highlights that continuity with preexilic life is important to the *golah* community. This same people who had seen pre-exilic life would be those in Ezra 3:2–3 making comparisons between the pre-exilic life and now and desiring to build the altar in the "correct" way—how it was before the exile. The last verse mentions that other people from afar could hear the sound of the *golah* community but could not distinguish the shouts of joy and the weeping (Ezra 3:13). This last verse then implies that while the *golah* community has been undertaking the building project—laying the foundation of the temple and celebrating—others (non-*golah*) were not part of them and were simply overhearers/onlookers.

Summary on Laying the Foundations (Ezra 3:1–13)

In this section, the *golah* group is identified mainly by the term Israelites. The *golah* group is described as continuing pre-exilic life by performing "correct cult" as was carried out in pre-exilic time—such as building the altar on its original site according to the law of Moses, observing festivals and burnt offerings as is written and prescribed (Ezra 3:2–4). The note of the emotions of those who had seen the first temple and now the foundation of the new one (Ezra 3:10–12) also highligts connection with pre-exilic life. Another description of the *golah* group is "all those who came back from the captivity to Jerusalem" (Ezra 3:8), implying that the *golah* community is mainly composed of those who had been exiled to Babylon and return.

The "other" people are identified by the phrase peoples of the lands. There is no further information for specific identification, thus the phrase seems to refer to any or all people who are not part of the *golah* group, who had been dwelling in the land when the *golah* group arrived. These "other" people caused dread for the *golah* people (Ezra 3:3) and did not take part in the activities of the *golah* community, but were simply onlookers/overhearers (Ezra 3:13). The relationship between the *golah* and the "other" is clearly not amicable. Thus, as in the first section, this section too is interested primarily in the *golah* group. While the identification and description of the *golah* group are relatively well-presented, the "other" group is not properly identified. The "others" are also presented negatively as causing dread to the protagonist *golah* group. The *golah* group would continue to face adversity as they continue the temple project.

Ezra 4: Facing the Adversaries

Ezra 4 is the first account of real interaction between the *golah* group and the "other." In this passage, the relationship between the *golah* and the "other" is not just unfriendly but adversarial.

> When the adversaries of Judah and Benjamin heard that the *golah* community were building a temple to YHWH the God of Israel, they approached Zerubbabel and the heads of the families and said to them, "Let us build with you, because like you, we worship your God and we have been sacrificing to him since the days of Esarhaddon, the king of Assyria, who brought us here." But Zerubbabel, Jeshua and the rest of the heads of the families of Israel said to them, "(It is) not for you and us to build the house of our God, because we alone will build to YHWH the God of Israel, as king Cyrus, the king of Persia, has commanded us."
>
> Then the people of the land weakened the hands of the people of Judah, and they troubled them to build. They hired against them counsellors to frustrate their plan all the days of Cyrus, the king of Persia, until the reign of Darius, the king of Persia. (Ezra 4:1–5)

This passage will be studied in detail in chapter 2, so it will suffice here to comment briefly. As the *golah* group undertook the temple re-building work, they faced opposition, which is narrated in Ezra 4:1–5. The "other" group is identified as "adversaries of Judah and Benjamin," where Judah and Benjamin would stand for the *golah* community.[24] The designations for the "other" in 4:1–5 are simply "adversaries of Judah and Benjamin" and "people of the land," without further information for specific identification.

---

24. While here (Ezra 4:1) we have "Judah and Benjamin," later (Ezra 4:4), only Judah is mentioned. It seems that in Ezra 4:1, "Judah" and "Benjamin" are used as the names of the families, and in Ezra 4:4, Judah would be referring to the name of the province Judah/Yehud.

Identifications & Relationship of the *Golah* & the "Other"

The adversaries proposed to join in building the temple, claiming that they have been worshipping the God of the *golah* since they were brought to this land. The *golah* group, however, declined by claiming that they alone would build it, being the ones commanded by the king of Persia (Ezra 4:3). While the adversaries employed cultic terms to claim eligibility to build the temple together, the *golah* leaders denied them in legal terms (Ezra 1:3). It could be that the *golah* group understood Cyrus's order to be addressed exclusively to them, and they were afraid to disobey it (Ezra 1:2–4). Also, while they did not openly deny the claim of the adversaries' worshipping the same God, it does not necessarily mean they accepted it. They seemed to be at their utmost care to keep their group intact, and stick to what (they thought) was right. It is clear that the *golah* community do not want these "adversaries" to join in the temple building.

The following verse (Ezra 4:4) states that the people of the land weakened the hands of the people of Judah and caused troubles such that they could not continue the building work. The text does not say how the people of the land weakened the *golah* group's building work, but the next verse offers an explanation. Ezra 4:5 states that counsellors were hired against the *golah* group, such that they could not continue to build the temple, which could only be resumed in the reign of Darius (also see Ezra 4:24). Ezra 4:6–24 further narrates three accusation letters written against the *golah* community. First, an accusation was submitted to Ahasuerus (Xerxes) (Ezra 4:6). Second, Bishlam, Mithredath, Tabeel and their associates wrote to king Artaxerxes (Ezra 4:7). No further details of these two letters are known. A third letter of accusation is from the officials Rehum, Shimshai, and others, to Artaxerxes (Ezra 4:8–10).[25] After noting the different oppositions the *golah* experienced, the author concludes that the work on the

---

25. This third letter is explained further in Ezra 4:11–16, where reference is made on the building of the walls and the city, rather than the temple itself (Ezra 4:12). This may seem problematic and questionable on the chronology of historical events. However, it is quite possible that the author is adding the series of other oppositions and difficulties the *golah* community experienced in their journey of rebuilding the house of God—of the temple and later the city walls, and thus not strictly concerned with historical chronology. This section of letters with some digressions from the time of the current narrative and mentioning future references such as the city wall could be understood as brackets or footnotes of an ancient author. See Williamson, *Ezra, Nehemiah*, 57, 63.

On the "house of God," Eskenazi convincingly argues that the "house of God" in Ezra–Nehemiah comprises not only the temple but including the city and walls. See Eskenazi, *In an Age of Prese*, 53–57.

house of God could not be continued until the second year of Darius (Ezra 4:24; cf. 4:5).

Summary on Facing Adversaries (Ezra 4:1–24)

In this section, the *golah* group is identified as "Judah and Benjamin," and accordingly, the "other" are "adversaries of Judah and Benjamin" (Ezra 4:1). The term "adversaries" itself carries a negative connotation. Wishing to join the temple building work, these "adversaries" claimed to worship the same God. But they were denied by the *golah* group, who claimed that they alone would build, as the ones authorized by King Cyrus (Ezra 1:3). Another designation of the "other" is "people of the land," who discouraged the *golah* people and caused troubles for their work. Other "other" people are the officials who wrote the accusation letters (Ezra 4:7–10). All "other" people in this section are portrayed negatively.

For both terms for the "other"—adversaries and people of the land—there is no further information about who they are referring to. No explicit reason is given in the text about why the "adversaries" are called so and who precisely they are. Similarly, the term people of the land is without further information for identification. It seems then that all other people, officials or the general populace, who are not part of the returned *golah*, are treated together in one broad "other" group, and are in unfriendly and oppositional relationship with the *golah* group.

The temple building work ceased because of opposition, but it would resume with the inspiration from prophets.

Ezra 5:1–6:15: Resumption and Completion of the Temple

Ezra 5:1–6:15 narrates the resumption of the building work until its completion in the sixth year of the reign of King Darius, though not without hurdles (6:15). As a result of the prophesying of Haggai and Zechariah, the building work resumed, led by Zerubbabel and Jeshua, and with the support of the prophets (Ezra 5:1–2). This implies that YHWH was behind the life and activities of the *golah*, a theme which has already been seen from the beginning of the narrative, where those who returned are introduced as those stirred by YHWH (Ezra 1:5).

Not long after the resumption of the work, the community faced some query from the Persian officials: "At the same time, Tattenai, the governor of Beyond the River, Shethar-bozenai and their associates came to them and said to them: 'Who gave you command to build this house and finish this structure?'" (Ezra 5:3). Here, the "others" are officials who questioned the work of the *golah* community, designated as "Jews"[26]—Tattenai, the governor of the province Beyond the River, Shethar-bozenai and their associates. They asked if they had persmission to build the temple and also for the names of those who were building (Ezra 5:3). This query may not necessarily be an act of confrontation. It could simply be that they were carrying out their duty as officials to confirm that the builders had permission to build. The letter they wrote to king Darius is also largely a report of the speech of the *golah* people about their story (Ezra 5:7b–17). Still, such queries could end undesirably for the *golah* people. However, God protected them and they were not stopped from the work while Darius's reply was received (Ezra 5:5). Once again, the involvement of YHWH in the life and work of the *golah* community is seen (cf. Ezra 1:5; 5:1).

In the letter of Tattenai and his colleagues, the self-description of the Jews is reported: as the servants of the God of heaven and earth, rebuilding the house (of God) that was built many years ago by a great king of Israel (Ezra 5:11). The destruction of the house and their exile are attributed to their ancestors' mistake of making God angry (Ezra 5:12). This self-description highlights two important characteristics of the *golah* community: that they are YHWH's people and that they are the continuation of the preexilic Israel.

Tattenai and his colleagues also asked king Darius to search for Cyrus's edict, which gave them permission to build the house of God (5:13, 17). In response, Darius searched and found the decree of Cyrus, which is cited in Ezra 6:1–5, though with some variations from the one cited earlier in Ezra 1:3. The one in Ezra 1:3 asks those in exile to return to Jersualem to build the house, while the one in Ezra 6:3 describes mainly the building, not the builders. The emphasis on the permission and details of the building in Ezra 6:3 could be because it was mainly aimed to answer the question of the Persian officials whether they had the permission to build the temple (Ezra 5:3b).[27] This passage then confirms them as the ones in-charge of the

---

26. The protagonist *golah* group is identified by the term "Jews" in the Aramaic section (Ezra 4:8–6:18).

27. There are other differences, such as more details are found here in 6:3–4 which

building. Earlier in the narrative the *golah* group has stated also that they are the ones authorized by Cyrus (Ezra 4:3).

Having found the edict, Darius even asked Tattenai, Shethar-bozenai and their associates not to trouble them but rather to aid in this building project (Ezra 6:6–9). Darius also warned that anyone altering his decree would be punished (Ezra 6:11). Thus the building work continued and was completed on the third of the month Adar in the sixth year of the reign of king Darius (Ezra 6:15).[28] The completion of the temple is credited to three things: the command of the God of Israel, re-energizing through the prophecy of Haggai and Zechariah, and the supportive edicts of the Persian kings of Cyrus, Darius and Artaxerxes (Ezra 6:14).[29] Thus, God (YHWH) is central to the completion of the temple and the Persian kings are also supportive.

Summary on the Resumption and Completion of the Temple (Ezra 5:1–6:15)

This section narrates how the temple rebuilding work was resumed and eventually completed. In this section (in Aramaic), the *golah* community is mostly identified by the term Jews/Judeans (Ezra 5:1, 5; 6:8, 14). The building resumed only through the prophecy of Haggai and Zechariah (Ezra 5:1) and when they were questioned by the Persian officials, their God protected them (Ezra 5:5). The *golah* community also identified themselves as "servants of God" (Ezra 5:11) and as responsible to mend the mistake of their ancestors by rebuilding the temple (Ezra 5:12). Thus, YHWH continues to be the central figure for the *golah* group and they are seen as the continuation of preexilic Israel.

---

are not found in 1:3, such as the measurements of the temple, the expenses to be paid by the palace, and such. It is probable that the edict is not reproduced in its entirety, neither here nor in Ezra 1:3, but just the relevant parts for each context are extracted.

28. The sixth year of Darius is 515 BCE, the month of Adar is the twelfth month, so it could be around 12 March 515 BCE (Clines, *Ezra, Nehemiah, Esther*, 94).

29. The prophecy of Haggai and Zechariah around the date of the completion of the temple (515 BCE) is doubtful, since Haggai's activity was around 520 BCE and that of Zechariah would have ended around 518 BCE (Clines, *Ezra, Nehemiah, Esther*, 95). Thus, it could be a generalization or a reference back to the prophecy of Haggai and Zechariah to resume the work when the work was halted because of adversities (Ezra 4:4–5; 5:1).

The inclusion of Artaxerxes is also questionable, whose reign only comes later (464–423 BCE). Yet, it could be in anticipation of Artaxerxes's support later towards the temple (such as Ezra 7:15–24, 27; see also Ezra 9:9). See Williamson, *Ezra, Nehemiah*, 83–84.

Identifications & Relationship of the *Golah* & the "Other"

The "others" in this section are named Persian officials, Tattenai, Shethar-bozenai and their associates. They are not necessarily portrayed negatively—they came and questioned whether the *golah* group had permission to build the temple and they reported back to Darius. There is no explicit sign of hostility in their interaction with the *golah* group or in their communication with Darius about them (Ezra 5:3, 7–17).

Ezra 6:16–22: Temple Dedication and Passover Celebration

Dedication of the Temple
(Ezra 6:16–18)

> The Israelites, the priests and the Levites, and the rest of the *golah* did the dedication of this house of God with joy. And they offered for the dedication of this house of God one hundred bulls, two hundred rams, four hundred lambs, and twelve male-goats as sin-offering for all Israel according the tribes of Israel. (Ezra 6:16–17)

As the temple building work was completed, the *golah* community had a joyful dedication. Here the *golah* community is called "Israelites."[30] The participants at the dedication are listed, as usual in the book of Ezra, as: the lay Israelites, the priests and the Levites (Ezra 6:16; cf. 3:8). Interestingly here, however, the list extends to include one more group: "the rest of the *golah*." If the "Israelites" will represent lay members, who would the "rest of the *golah*" be referring to? Is it simply a redundant repetition?[31] Or, does it imply that not everyone who had returned from the exile participated in the rebuilding of the temple and "the rest" is to refer to them joining the dedication?[32] Or, are the "rest of the *golah*" not exile returnees but others who now have joined the *golah* community? The text does not answer the question explicitly. However, from the context where non-*golah* people are welcome into the Passover celebration later (Ezra 6:21) it makes the most sense that some non-returnees joined the temple dedication.

---

30. In other parts of the Aramaic section, "Jews/Judeans" is used. As Clines suggests, "Israel" at the completion and dedication of the temple would imply how the *golah* group understand themselves to stand for the whole of Israel, and also different from how others would refer them ("Jews") (Clines, *Ezra, Nehemiah, Esther*, 96).

31. Grabbe, *Ezra-Nehemiah*, 25.

32. Batten, *Ezra and Nehemiah*, 150.

That twelve goats were sacrificed according to the number of the tribes of Israel (Ezra 6:17) does not necessarily mean that all twelve tribes were present at the dedication to make the sacrifices themselves. It may simply mean that the *golah* community remembered their fellow Israelites wherever they were.[33] More significantly, it implies that the *golah* community viewed themselves as representing the whole of Israel.[34]

After the dedication of the temple, they appointed priests and Levites "as written in the book of Moses" (Ezra 6:18). There is no further specific information on the book of Moses, and it could be generally understood as the teachings of Moses (cf. Ezra 3:3). But more important than the identification of the book of Moses is their desire to appoint leaders and do cultic activities "correctly" (as also in Ezra 3:3). The reference to the preexilic figure Moses implies the desire of the *golah* community to follow and maintain preexilic ways, thus highlighting again their community as the continuation of preexilic Israel. After dedicating the temple, the Passover was celebrated (Ezra 6:19–22).

Celebration of the Passover
(Ezra 6:19–22)

> On the fourteenth (day) of the first month, the *golah* community[35] celebrated the Passover. For both the priests and the Levites have purified themselves, all of them are pure. And they slaughtered the Passover for all the *golah* community, for their brothers the priests, and for themselves. The Israelites ate—those who had returned from the exile and all those who had separated themselves from the uncleanness of the nations of the land to (join) them, to worship YHWH, God of Israel. (Ezra 6:19–22)

This passage about the Passover celebration will be analyzed in detail in chapter 3, so a brief examination is adequate here. This passage is unique because it expresses the participation of non-*golah* in the Passover. The passage begins with the statement that the *golah* community, identified as "the sons of the *golah*," celebrated the Passover (Ezra 6:19). Later, those who partook in the Passover are listed (Ezra 6:21): first, the Israelites who

---

33. Batten, *Ezra and Nehemiah*, 150.
34. Clines, *Ezra, Nehemiah, Esther*, 97; Williamson, *Ezra, Nehemiah*, 84.
35. Literally, "sons of the *golah*." I translate it as "*golah* community" to reflect the whole community, which is what is meant here.

had returned from the exile, and second, all who had joined them to worship YHWH by separating themselves from the uncleanness of the nations of the land. The first group of participants, "Israelites," needs no further explanation; it is those who are already members of the *golah* community. The second group is questionable, as they are simply described as "all those who had separated themselves from the uncleanness of the nations of the land and join them to seek YHWH."

Some argue that the phrase "all those who had separated themselves from the uncleanness of the nations of the land and join them to worship YHWH" refer to none other than the Israelites themselves. For instance, Thiessen argues that the conjunction *wĕ* here should be translated epexegetically as "that is," rather than an "and," such that the phrase is a description of the same subject "Israelites" and not an introduction of another group of people.[36] While grammatical rules may allow translation of *wĕ* in that manner in some cases, there is no strong evidence in this context to translate it that way. No other place in Ezra is such a description made for the already existing *golah* community members. In fact, listing of people acccording to different categories is common in the book of Ezra (e.g., Ezra 2:2b, 36, 40; 3:12; 7:7; 9:1), and this passage would be understood in that manner too. From the description "all those who joined them (the *golah*) by separating themselves from the uncleanness of the nations of the land," it would be referring to those who, like the *golah* people, have kept themselves apart from "uncleanness" that is unacceptable to YHWH and the *golah* community.[37] Also, they joined them to worship YHWH. As such, they have met the expectation to be a part of the *golah* community. With no further information about their specific identity, it can only be said that it could be anyone—non-exiled Israelites or non-Israelites.

The allowance of "others" in partaking the Passover implies welcoming them into their community as well. It must be noted, however, that it is not an open invitation to all random people. It is those who have met the expectation of what it takes to be part of the *golah* community who are welcomed, those who have separated themselves from what is unacceptable to YHWH and the *golah* community and join the *golah* group to seek YHWH.

---

36. Thiessen, "Function of a Conjunction." His arguments will be discussed further in chapter 3.

37. The meaning of this clause will be examined in detail in chapter 3.

This passage concludes by giving credit to YHWH for inclining the heart of the king[38] to turn toward and support the *golah* community in their temple building work. The Ezra narrative actually begins with a similar theme of YHWH inspiring Cyrus to allow exiled Jews to return to Jerusalem and start the rebuilding work (Ezra 1:1). Thus, YHWH is the central figure behind the *golah* community and their building project—stirring up the hearts of people to return (Ezra 1:1, 5), inspiring the prophets Haggai and Zechariah to boost the *golah* community to resume the building work after it was halted by adversity (Ezra 5:1), and inclining even a foreign king's heart to allow the temple to be completed (Ezra 6:22).

Summary on Temple Dedication and Passover Celebration (Ezra 6:16–22)

Unlike previous sections that record the hardships of the *golah* community—such as being in fear of "others" (Ezra 3:3) and facing adversaries (Ezra 4:1–4), this section narrates the accomplishments and celebrations of the *golah* community. The *golah* community is referred to as Israelites (literally "sons of Israel" [Ezra 6:16, 21]) and the *golah* community (literally "sons of the *golah*" [Ezra 6:16, 19–20]). This passage is also distinctive in that the "other/s" are presented positively, as joining the *golah* community to partake the Passover meal and to worship YHWH, implying being welcomed into the community (Ezra 6:21). Evidently, these "other" people have joined the *golah* community to worship YHWH after meeting the criterion of separating themselves from what is unacceptable to be a *golah* community member.

The criterion to separate from the uncleanness of the nations of the land has been implied from the outset of the narrative, and the characteristics of the *golah* community also revolve around this criterion. They view themselves to be exclusively YHWH's people (e.g., Ezra 1:3; 4:3), the ones authorized by Cyrus to rebuild the house of YHWH (Ezra 1:3; 4:3; 5:11),

---

[38]. The text says "king of Assyria," when it should obviously be "king of Persia." It could be a scribal error. Or it could be that the author was using the title king of Assyria "as a stereotyped description of a foreign ruler" and to refer "to a title that had for a long time in history inspired fear in the hearts of the Jews" (Williamson, *Ezra, Nehemiah*, 85; Fensham, *Ezra, Nehemiah*, 97). But what is of interest here is not the historical correctness of the narrative but rather the claim that YHWH is the one at work over everything, including using the imperial powers for the good of the *golah* community.

the ones following cult "correctly" (in keeping the law of Moses/YHWH/ God [Ezra 3:2; 6:18]), as ones responsible to "fix" the mistake of their ancestors (Ezra 5:11) and thereby the ones continuing preexilic Israel (Ezra 1:3; 3:2; 5:11; 6:17). Central also in this passage is that not only *all* of the *golah* community but even some "other" people participated in the temple dedication and the Passover celebrations (Ezra 6:16, 21). This section is followed by the account of the *golah* community with Ezra as its main leader (Ezra 7–10).

Ezra 7–8: More Return to Jerusalem, Led by Ezra

The rest of the narrative (Ezra 7–10, Neh 8) captures the life of the *golah* community under the leadership of Ezra.[39] The section begins with the introduction of Ezra: his genealogy and his scribal skill in the law; he came to Jerusalem during the reign of Artaxerxes.[40] What is noticeable immediately is that YHWH is the true cause for the return of Ezra.

> This Ezra came up from Babylon; he is a scribe, skilled in the law of Moses which YHWH the God of Israel had given. The king granted him all his request as the favor of YHWH his God was upon him. Some of the Israelites and some of the priests, Levites, singers, gatekeepers and temple servants came up to Jerusalem on the seventh year of king Artaxerxes. (Ezra 7:6-7)

The list of those who return with Ezra—some of the Israelites, some of the priests, Levites, singers, gatekeepers and temple servants (Ezra 7:7) highlights cultic and temple personnel, so it signifies that the temple in

---

39. Ezra 7–10 is commonly known as Ezra Memoir, with some parts narrated in the third-person (Ezra 7:1-11; 8:35-36; 10:1-44) and other parts in the first-person (Ezra 7:27–8:34; 9:1-15). To this may be added Neh 8 (or more precisely, Neh 7:73b—8:18), which is also an account of Ezra in the third-person. Even though these parts are in different person forms, the stories follow a coherent theme. See Klein, *Ezra & Nehemiah*, 715.

40. Artaxerxes here is mostly assumed to be Artaxerxes I, thus Ezra's arrival would be 458 BCE (seventh year of Artaxerxes I; Ezra 7:6-7), leaving about fifty-seven years gap from the last event of temple dedication (515 BCE). If it was Artaxerxes II, Ezra's arrival would be much later, around 398 BCE, leaving an even larger gap. It is more natural to assume Artaxerxes I, someone who is already mentioned in the narrative (Ezra 4:7; 6:14). And the gap of about fifty-seven years between the last account in Ezra 6 and the beginning of Ezra 7 may not necessarily mean that the author did not know anything about the period, but rather that there was no event significant and interesting enough for the author. See Blenkinsopp, *Ezra-Nehemiah*, 135.

Jerusalem would be functioning. The passage also states that the king granted all of Ezra's request mainly because the favor of YHWH (literally, "hand of YHWH") was upon Ezra (Ezra 7:6).[41] Thus, YHWH is the root source of the life of the *golah* community. Similarly, Ezra's journey back to and arrival in Jerusalem are also credited to YHWH (Ezra 7:9, literally, "because of the good hand of his God"). In fact, YHWH is not only in-charge of the *golah* community but also over the Persians such that if they do not obey God's order for the temple, they will incur wrath upon themselves (Ezra 7:23). Ezra gave all credit to YHWH, God of their fathers, for inclining the king and officials' hearts, and as a result of which he could gather some leaders to go with him to Jerusalem (Ezra 7:27–28).

As in Ezra 1 where Cyrus permitted the *golah* to return to Jerusalem (Ezra 1:2–4), here Artaxerxes made a similar decree allowing a return to Jerusalem (Ezra 7:13–26): "I make a decree that anyone in my kingdom from the people of Israel, priests and Levites who volunteers to go to Jerusalem with you may go" (Ezra 7:13). Similar to Cyrus's decree (Ezra 1:2–4), Artaxerxes's decree also calls out to those who are willing, to return. On the other hand, unlike in Cyrus's decree where the people were to return and rebuild the temple, in Artaxerxes's decree the people were to return and "rebuild the community." Notable also is the more specific nature of Artaxerxes edict than that of Cyrus. Artaxerxes's edict mentions the priests and Levites besides the lay people, implying that they were returning for service in the temple. The edict also conveys the king of Persia, the "other," as very supportive of the *golah* community: not only sending Ezra to inquire of Judah and Jerusalem according to the law of his (Ezra's) God (Ezra 7:14), but he and his advisers also donated freewill offerings for the God of Israel in Jerusalem and allowed Ezra to look for silver and gold throughout the province of Babylon (Ezra 7:15–16). Ezra would then return to deliver vessels for service in the house of God (Ezra 7:19). Furthermore, any other needs were to be provided from the royal treasuries (Ezra 7:20), and no tax

---

41. The "hand of YHWH" could mean protection, strength, or power (Exod 9:3, protection over the animals of Israelites; 1 Kgs 18:46, strength or favor upon Elijah; 2 Kgs 3:15, presence or inspiration upon Elisha to prophesy). In the context here, the "hand of YHWH" would mean YHWH's favor was upon Ezra. The pronominal suffix "upon him" is open in that "him" could signify Ezra or the king; that is, the hand/favor of YHWH was upon Ezra or the king. It makes more sense if it stands for Ezra, but the possibility of it referring to the king is not nullified. Either way, whether it signifies Ezra or the king, the central idea remains unchanged—that the true source of favor and granting of Ezra's requests actually comes from YHWH, not simply the king of Persia.

was to be imposed on the tributes nor on those serving in the house of God (Ezra 7:24).

Thus, the centrality of YHWH is stressed again in Ezra 7. The community would be judged whether they follow cult "correctly," that is, according to God's law (Ezra 7:14). The leader, Ezra himself, was equipped with that law (Ezra 7:6). He diligently learned the law and his purpose in Jerusalem was to teach and lead the people according to that same law (Ezra 7:10, 11b). This implies the centrality of YHWH in the life of the *golah* community. Their life depended on their obedience to YHWH by obeying YHWH's law.

Ezra 8 continues with the list of those who return to Jerusalem with Ezra. There are a few important things to notice in this list. Ezra made sure that both priests and Levites, that is, cultic leaders, returned with him to Jerusalem (Ezra 8:15), implying the importance of cult for the *golah* community. Also, while the permission came from the Persian king, the ability to gather capable people to return and the safe journey were attributed to YHWH's favor (literally, "hand of God" [Ezra 8:18, 22, 31]). As they arrive, the first thing Ezra and his group did was to offer burnt offerings (Ezra 8:35; cf. 3:3, 6). Ezra and his group offered twelve bulls for *all* Israel (Ezra 8:35; cf. 6:17).

Summary on More Return, Led by Ezra
(Ezra 7–8)

This section Ezra 7–8 on the permission, preparation and return of Ezra with some people to Jerusalem presents some characteristics of the protagonist *golah* group. The *golah* group are keen to follow YHWH God and the law of YHWH. Ezra, who was skilled in the law, was sent to inquire if the *golah* community was living according to the law of Moses/YHWH/God (Ezra 7:14), and then to teach those who did not know the law (Ezra 7:25). They sought YHWH before they started their journey (Ezra 8:21) and the first thing they did on arrival in Jerusalem was offer burnt offerings (Ezra 8:35). YHWH is the real source of favor and protection for the *golah* community, though it may be realized through the Persian king and officials (Ezra 7:6b, 27–28; 8:18, 21–22, 31). As with the first return (Ezra 1–2), the return led by Ezra has cultic purposes and YHWH and YHWH's law are central in the life of the *golah* community.

The "other" people mentioned are the Persian king Artaxerxes and his advisers (Ezra 7:1, 7, 11–12, 27; 8:1). They are portrayed positively. The decree of Artaxerxes presents him as very supportive of the *golah* group and willing to obey the commands of God (YHWH), particularly in regard to the house of God in Jerusalem (Ezra 7:23). The king, as well as his advisers, even contributed freewill offerings for the God of Israel who is in Jerusalem (Ezra 7:15). As Ezra and the team arrived in Jerusalem, measures to rebuild the community began, starting with the reading and interpretation of the law.

Neh 8; Ezra 9–10:
Rebuilding the *Golah* Community under Ezra

In this section (Neh 8; Ezra 9–10), the protagonist *golah* group is identified by terms such as people (Neh 8:1, 3, 5, 12–13, 16), "Israelites" (Ezra 9:1; 10:1–2, 5), "Judah and Benjamin" (Ezra 10:9; cf. 4:1), assembly (*qāhāl*) (Neh 8:2, 17; Ezra 10:1, 8, 12, 14), the *golah* (Ezra 9:4; 10:6; "sons of the *golah*" [Ezra 10:7]). The "other" people are designated by two terms: the peoples of the lands and foreign women (Ezra 9:1, 2; 10:2, 3, 14).

As Ezra arrived in Jerusalem, the first measure to rebuild the community was to teach and implement the law to the people as was commissioned (Ezra 7:25). The reading of the law is narrated in Neh 8, and later its implementation is narrated in Ezra 9–10. But before delving into the reading of the law, a brief comment is called for in regard to the position of Neh 8.

That Neh 8 fits well within the Ezra Memoir is easy to observe.[42] First, Neh 8 is about the reading and obeying of the law, which is also the main

---

42. As noted by several commentators, the chronology of Neh 8 in Nehemiah makes less sense. Nehemiah received permission from Artaxerxes on first month of twentieth year of Artaxerxes II (445 BCE) (Neh 2:1), walls completed on twenty-fifth day of sixth month (still twentieth year) (Neh 6:15), followed by events of Neh 7–9 apparently in the same year—that is, the law reading on the first and second days of seventh month (8:2, 13), the festival of booths on fifteenth to twenty-secondth days (8:18) of seventh month, then penitential assembly followed on twenty-fourth day of seventh month (9:1). This chronology raises question why Ezra (who came to Jerusalem on seventh year of Artaxerxes I, 458 BCE) waited thirteen years to carry out the law reading. And also, it makes more sense that the people would come to realization of their unfaithfulness (beginning of Ezra 9) after some kind of study of the law (Neh 8). Thus, from literary analysis and chronology, Neh 8 fits better between Ezra 8 (that ends with the arrival of Ezra) and Ezra 9 (which begins with the report about some *golah* community who did not live up to the expectation of the law). See Clines, *Ezra, Nehemiah, Esther*, 180–81; Williamson, *Ezra, Nehemiah*, 283.

theme of Ezra 7–10. Secondly, Ezra, unlike in other parts of the book of Nehemiah, became, rather abruptly, the main character in Neh 8. Both in Ezra 7–10 and Neh 8, Ezra's leadership invites action from the people (Ezra 9:1; Neh 8:1), which is quite distinct for Ezra. Thus their literary style is the same. Within the Ezra Memoir, Neh 8 fits best between Ezra 8 and 9.[43] It makes most sense that the people would come to realize that their failure to keep themselves apart from "other" people was an unfaithfulness (Ezra 9) after having studied the law, which happens in Neh 8.

Nehemiah 8 shows the *golah* community as united and eager to follow the law of Moses. The people gathered as one and asked Ezra to read to them from the law (Neh 8:1); the ears of the people were attentive to the law as it was read (Neh 8:3b); the people also worshipped and had great respect to the law—the people stood up as Ezra opened the scroll of law (Neh 8:5), and they responded with "Amen" and raised hands, prostrating themselves before YHWH (Neh 8:6). Explanations of the law were also given by leaders

---

43. On the position of Neh 8 within Ezra Memoir, there are two main arguments. First, that Neh 8 fits between Ezra 8 and 9. Second, that it fits at the end, after Ezra 10. To me, Neh 8 fits better between Ezra 8 and 9 than after Ezra 10. In Neh 8, as the people listened to the law and its explanations, they became very sad and were weeping, perhaps realizing their failure to keep the law (Neh 8:9b, 10b, 11b). Ezra 9 then begins with the phrase "when these were over," which could imply the reading and explanation of the law to the people (Neh 8), and continues with some from the *golah* community reporting to Ezra about the failure of (some of) the *golah* community (Ezra 9:1). The people also came up with resolutionary actions "in accordance with the counsel of the lord (that is, Ezra) and those who tremble at the commandment of God and the law will be obeyed" (Ezra 10:3). Such actions—realization of the failures to keep the law and resolutionary measures—anticipate some kind of study and understanding of the law beforehand, which is what is happening in Neh 8 under leadership of Ezra (and some other laypeople and Levites). Finally, positioning Neh 8 between Ezra 8 and 9 also results in a smooth chronology—Ezra arrived in the fifth month (Ezra 7:8), read the law in the seventh month (Neh 7:72b; 8:2), and the intermarriage was dealt in the ninth month (Ezra 10:9). See Blenkinsopp, *Ezra-Nehemiah*, 45.

The alternative view that Neh 8 should be after Ezra 10, thus concluding Ezra Memoir, gets its support mainly from 1 Esdras that arranges it that way. This argument posits that it makes more sense that the author (Chronicler) would like to end his work with a more festive and joyful situation. This view also assumes that Ezra is presenting a new set of law in Neh 8, as such it is not so related with the actions of Ezra 9–10, which also have the law as its central basis. This view does not hold strong, as Williamson argues, since the arrangement in 1 Esdras, being a "secondary compilation," should not be taken as the basis. Also it is now commonly viewed that Ezra is not necessarily bringing a new law but that the people have neglected it or perhaps Ezra was just presenting a fresh interpretation. See Williamson, *Ezra, Nehemiah*, 284–85.

For more discussions on the positioning of Neh 8, see Blenkinsopp, *Ezra-Nehemiah*, 44–46, 284–85; Williamson, *Ezra, Nehemiah*, 283–86.

and Levites so that the people will understand (Neh 8:7–9). On the second day, the heads of the clans of all the people, the priests and the Levites gathered again before Ezra to study the law (Neh 8:13). But not only did they study, the people also followed the law of Moses. As they learned of the command to dwell in booths during the festival of the seventh month,[44] they fulfilled it right away (Neh 8:14–17).

The law is vital for the rebuilding of the *golah* community, as also seen in its formation earlier in the narrative, such as having the altar, sacrifices and festivals correctly according to the law of Moses (Ezra 3). As common in the book of Ezra, the connection with preexilic life appears here again—they were fulfilling the stipulation of the law again after it was last fulfilled during the time of Joshua (Neh 8:17). The centrality of the law in the life of the community may be best seen in the statement that the people celebrated with choice foods and drinks because they have understood the law (Neh 8:9–12). Having understood the law, they now can realize what is lawful and acceptable to YHWH and what is not.

Ezra 9 then follows with some leaders of the *golah* community reporting to Ezra about the unfaithfulness (*ma'al*) the community has committed in failing to keep themselves apart from "other" people and intermarrying with them, such that the "holy seed" has mixed with the peoples of the lands (Ezra 9:1–2).

> When these were done, the leaders approached me, saying, "The people of Israel, the priests and the Levites have not kept themselves apart from the peoples of the lands, with their abominations as the Canaanites, the Hittites, the Perizzites, the Jebusites, the Ammonites, the Moabites, the Egyptians and the Amorites. For they have taken some of their daughters for themselves and their sons, and the holy seed has mixed itself with the peoples of the lands, and the hand of the leaders and the rulers are foremost in this unfaithfulness. (Ezra 9:1–2)

Some of the *golah*, both lay people and clergy, have failed to maintain their core requirement of being a *golah* community member—keeping themselves apart, separating themselves from the peoples of the lands (Ezra 9:1). More precisely, they transgressed by taking some women from the peoples of the lands as their wives and as their daughters-in-law. In fact,

---

44. Lev 23:33–44 (particularly verses 40, 42–43). Other references of the seventh month festival are seen in Exod 23:16; 34:22; Num 29:12–38.

Identifications & Relationship of the *Golah* & the "Other"

the leaders themselves are reported to be involved in this unfaithfulness (Ezra 9:2).[45]

One core way the *golah* community understand themselves is as the holy seed (Ezra 9:2). "Holy seed" in the current context would best be understood in the sense of being set apart for YHWH or belonging to YHWH.[46] Such an understanding also goes in line with being expected to "keep themselves apart" from the peoples of the lands (Ezra 9:1). The *golah* community is often evaluated by whether or not they have kept themselves apart from "other" people (Ezra 6:21; 9:1). The overriding theme of the book of Ezra is that the *golah* group is a "set apart" group, not to mingle with "other" people (e.g., Ezra 3:3; 4:3; 6:21). Thus, the *golah* group as a "holy seed" are set apart for YHWH, set apart from "other" people.

According to the text, the problem with these peoples of the lands was their abominations. Their abominable actions were like those of the Canaanites, the Hittites, the Perizzites, the Jebusites, the Ammonites, the Moabites, the Egyptians, and the Amorites (Ezra 9:2).[47] The text does not spell out what the "abominations" (*tô'ēbâ*) of these peoples of the lands are, but a general meaning of the term can be drawn from the larger context of the Ezra narrative as well as outside. The term "abominations," particularly when used in association with non-Israelites, refers to the idolatrous and unethical nature (such as sexual immorality) of non-YHWH worshippers.[48]

---

45. The "hands of the rulers are foremost in this unfaithfulness" could mean that they are the ones who fail in this act first. Or, it could simply mean that they are involved in the act or they approved such acts. There is no way to know if the leaders committed this unfaithfulness first and others followed. It is safe to say that even the leaders, who should have known better, were involved in this unfaithfulness.

The term for unfaithfulness, *ma'al*, mostly expresses unfaithfulness against God/YHWH (Lev 5:15; Ezek 17:20; 39:26; Josh 22:22; 1 Chr 9:1; 2 Chr 29:19), though it can also express faithfulness against other humans (e.g., Job 21:34). In this context also, it is clearly implying that this unfaithfulness of the *golah* is truly against their God, YHWH, who is truly the source of their provisions and life.

46. Ezra 9–10, including terms such as "holy seed," will be discussed in detail in chapter 4.

47. As these nations no longer thrived at this time, it is best to take this collection of nations as stereotyped nations. The list of nations also does not match any other collection, neither of Deut 7:1; 23:4, 8, nor of Exod 34:11.

48. For example, in several contexts, abominations/abominable actions refer to cultic aberration such as idolatry (Deut 7:25; 18:9–12; 20:18; Jer 44:4–5; Ezek 8:6–10, 15–16), in other contexts it references sexual immorality (Lev 18:22) or crossing social or cultural boundaries (such as: no dress exchange between man and woman [Deut 22:5]; Egyptians cannot eat with Israelites [Gen 43:32]). In other instances, abomination refers to things

The peoples of the lands would be following cultic and unethical lifestyles like the nations they are compared to, and such acts are not acceptable to YHWH or the *golah* community.

In response to the report of the transgression of the *golah* community, Ezra tore his garments and pulled out his hairs from head and beard and sat in desolation (Ezra 9:3); then, some from the *golah* group gathered around Ezra, who are described as "those who trembled at the word of God of Israel" (also see Ezra 10:3). They "trembled at the word of God" on account of their community's unfaithfulness and gathered around Ezra. The community has come to realize their unfaithfulness of not having kept themselves apart from the "others" and marrying their women. While it is not exactly clear what the "word of God" is to be identified with, this reference certainly resonates with the centrality of the law of God/YHWH for the *golah* community (cf. Ezra 7:6, 10, 14, 25). Despite their unfaithfulness, they were granted some favor: "But now, for a brief moment, there is favor from YHWH our God to leave us a remnant and to give us a stake in his holy place. Our God brightens our eyes and gives us a little regeneration in our slavery" (Ezra 9:8).

From Ezra 9:8, it can be seen that the other way the *golah* group perceived itself was as a "remnant" saved by God. As a remnant, however, they are not randomly saved, but purposefully to be the continuation of (pre-exilic) Israel, a theme seen throughout the narrative.[49] Thus, the self-understanding of the *golah* community as a "holy seed" and a "remnant" corelates. As set apart by God and saved as a remnant, they have responsibilities to maintain that status. Otherwise there might be no remnant left.

> After all that came upon us because of our evil deeds and our great guilt; yet you, since you our God have punished us less than our iniquities deserved and have given us a remnant as this, shall we break your commandments again and intermarry with the peoples of these abominations? Would you not be angry at us until you destroy us till there is no remnant or survivor at all? YHWH God of Israel, you are righteous, for we are spared as a remnant as

---

or persons/gods (food [Deut 14:3]; person/god [Isa 41:24]; land [Jer 2:7]; defect sheep [Deut 17:1]). In the context of Ezra 9:1–2, it will be implying the idolatrous nature of the peoples of the lands, not worshipping YHWH, just like the stereotypical ancient nations that are mentioned who were clearly idolatrous in the eyes of Israelites.

49. The meaning of the Hebrew term *pĕlêṭâ* is an escaped remnant, usually in reference to those who escaped from danger (Gen 32:9; 45:7; 2 Chr 12:7; 30:6; 2 Sam 15:14; 2 Kgs 19:30; Judg 21:17; Isa 37:31–32).

today. Here we are before you with our guilt, for no one can stand before you on this account. (Ezra 9:13–15)

Besides showing penitence physically (Ezra 9:3) Ezra also resorted to prayer (Ezra 9:6–15) where he recounted how they were in captivity because of the unfaithfulness of their forefathers. Still, God saved them as a remnant so they could not afford to be unfaithful again. Having come to the realization of their unfaithfulness, the community has to resolve this.

> While Ezra was praying, confessing, weeping and throwing himself in front of the house of God, a large number of men, women and children from the Israel assembly gathered to him, for the people wept bitterly.
>
> Then, Shecaniah, son of Jehiel from the descendants of Elam responded and said to Ezra, "We have been unfaithful to our God and we have married foreign women from the peoples of the land, but even now, there is hope for Israel on this account. Now, let us make a covenant with our God to send away all the women and those born from them, according to the advice of my lord and those who tremble at the commandment of our God. Let it be done according to the law. (Ezra 10:1–3)

Having cried over the unfaithfulness they committed, the *golah* community gathered around Ezra and proposed a resolution. Men, women as well as children are all listed as participating in this gathering, so the whole community took part in this act of remorse and resolution of their unfaithfulness (Ezra 10:1). As their unfaithfulness is the failure to keep themselves apart from "other" people and following abominable lifestyles unacceptable to YHWH and *golah* community, the resolution is also to get rid of them. This resolution would be in accordance with the law as well as Ezra and those who tremble at the commandment of God (Ezra 10:3; cf. 9:3). In order to carry out this resolution, a list of those who have married foreign women was produced (Ezra 10:18–43). The list includes names from all groups of the *golah* community—priestly families (Ezra 10:18–22), Levites (10:23), singers and gatekeepers (10:24), and lay Israelites (10:25–43). The list, and thus the Ezra narrative, ends abruptly with a corrupted text that simply reads: "All these married foreign women and some from them women had children" (Ezra 10:44b). So, from the text itself, it is not clear whether the foreign women and children borne from them were actually sent away. What is clear, however, is that the unfaithfulness of the *golah* community was taken seriously and dealt with accordingly.

Summary on Rebuilding the *Golah* Community (Neh 8; Ezra 9–10)

This section (Neh 8; Ezra 9–10) is about the rebuilding of the *golah* community under the leadership of Ezra. The terms used for the *golah* include "all the people" (Neh 8:1, 3, 5, 12–13), "Israel" (Ezra 9:1; 10:1–2, 5), assembly (Neh 8:17; Ezra 10:1, 8, 12, 14; "assembly of those who returned from the captivity" [Neh 8:2]), the *golah* (Ezra 9:4; 10:6), holy seed (Ezra 9:2), those who tremble at the word of God (Ezra 9:4; 10:3), and remnant (Ezra 9:8, 14–15). The terms used for the "other/s" are peoples of the lands (Ezra 9:1–2, 11; 10:2, 11), foreign women, and foreign women from the peoples of the land (Ezra 10:2, 10–11, 14, 17–18, 44).

In this section, the central theme for the *golah* community is the law— the law was read and studied as well as fulfilled (Neh 8), and according to the law, the unfaithfulness of the community was addressed (Ezra 9–10). The two core self-understandings of the *golah* community are being the "holy seed" and the "remnant" (Ezra 9:2, 8, 13–15). That is, they are the ones set apart for YHWH and from others to be the continuation of Israel. The unfaithfulness of the *golah* community is that they have not kept themselves apart from "others," designated by "peoples of the lands" and "foreign women," who have abominable lifestyles (Ezra 9:1–2). Thus, they tried to fix their mistake by sending away the foreign women from the peoples of the lands and their children (Ezra 10).

Conclusion

Surveying the book of Ezra, with particular attention to the characters and events, it can be seen that it is primarily and overwhelmingly about the protagonist *golah* group. While the protagonist *golah* group is properly identified, the "other" group/s are seldom identified, and are mentioned predominantly in respect to the *golah* group, positively or negatively.

From this survey, it is also discernable that the *golah* community is seen mainly as a cultic community. The return to the land to rebuild the temple originated from YHWH self, by stirring the spirit of Persian king Cyrus (Ezra 1:1) as well as the spirits of those who returned (Ezra 1:3). The first thing the *golah* community did when they arrived in Jerusalem was to make an altar and offer burnt offerings (Ezra 3:1–3; 8:35). Furthermore, eventhough the temple rebuilding work was halted by adversaries' interruption, it was resumed by the prophesying of the prophets who were inspired by God (Ezra 5:1–2). The *golah* community perceived themselves as the "holy seed" (Ezra 9:2)—set apart for YHWH or belonging to YHWH, and set apart from "others" and as the "remnant" (Ezra 9:8, 13–15)—saved purposefully by YHWH to perpetuate Israel into the future. The *golah* community is seen to be the continuation of preexilic Israel. The other main events of the *golah* community are also cultic, such as the dedication of the temple (Ezra 6:16), celebrating the Passover where they worshipped YHWH (Ezra 6:21), and reading and obeying the law (Neh 8; Ezra 9–10).

The "other" people, mainly described by terms such as people/s of the land/s, adversaries, and foreign women, are left with no possibility for further identification. On the other hand, some "other" people who are supportive of the *golah* community, particularly the Persian kings and officials, are named. Either way, however, these "other" people are not part of the *golah* community. Evidently, the "other" people comprise a broad group, made up of any non-*golah* member, non-exiled Jews or non-Jews. The main problem with the "other" people that is presented is that they have abominable lifestyles like typical non-Yahwistic nations (Ezra 9:1, 11, 14). For the *golah* community who is seen to be the "holy seed" and "remnant," to continue Israel into the future they have to keep themselves apart from abominable "others," unless they themselves have separated and joined the *golah* group to worship their God, YHWH (Ezra 6:21). We now turn to an analysis of particular events of encounter of the *golah* community and the "other," beginning with the first encounter in Ezra 4:1–5.

2

The First Encounter of the *Golah* and Their "Adversaries" (Ezra 4:1–5)

EZRA 4:1–5 NARRATES THE first obstruction the *golah* group faced as they began to build the temple. This incident happened in their first real encounter with the "other" in the book of Ezra.[1] Having had their first worship by setting up the altar and offering sacrifices and freewill offerings (Ezra 3:3–6), the *golah* group finally set out to build the temple. But, as they began the work of building the temple, "other" people—identified as the "adversaries of Judah and Benjamin"—proposed to build with them, claiming that they also worshipped the God of the *golah* (Ezra 4:1–2). The *golah* group leaders declined their proposal, stating that they alone, as charged by Cyrus, would build it (Ezra 4:3). After this encounter, the "other" group, designated by the phrase "people of the land" brought the building work of the *golah* group to a halt (Ezra 4:4). It is curious why "other" people were not allowed to participate in building the temple, and why they are designated as "adversaries" in the first place. It is also curious who these "other" people, designated by "adversaries" and "people of the land" might be.

From a literary analysis of the narrative it will be observed that while the text does not explicitly state the reason for the adversity, the conversation between the *golah* and the "other" in this passage exposes cult as the perceived difference between the two parties. The analysis also will

---

1. The first reference to the "other" in the book of Ezra is in Ezra 3:3, but it is just a report that the *golah* group was in dread of them.

illustrate that the narrative is primarily about the protagonist *golah* group and less about any "other" group. The antagonist "other" group receives no specific identifications and are often identified merely with respect to the protagonist *golah* group, whether positively or negatively.

The Event (Ezra 4:1–5)

[4:1] When the adversaries of Judah and Benjamin heard that the *golah* community[2] were building a temple to YHWH the God of Israel, [4:2] they approached Zerubbabel and the heads of the families[3] and they said to them, "Let us build with you, because like you, we worship your God and we have been sacrificing to him since the days of Esarhaddon,[4] the king of Assyria, who brought us here." [4:3] But Zerubbabel, Jeshua and the rest of the heads of the families of Israel said to them, "(It is) not for you and us to build the house of our God, because we alone will build to YHWH the God of Israel, as king Cyrus, the king of Persia, has commanded us."

[4:4] Then the people of the land weakened the hands of the people of Judah, and they troubled[5] them to build. [4:5] And they hired counsellors against them to frustrate their plan all the days of Cyrus, the king of Persia, until the reign of Darius, the king of Persia. (Ezra 4:1–5)

---

2. I translate it as "*golah* community" (literally, "sons of the *golah*") as that is meant here, not just male offpsrings of the *golah*. It is referring to the rebuilding of the temple taken up by the *golah* community.

3. The "heads of the families" (literally, "fathers") would be the lay leaders. See note 2 in chapter 1.

4. Esarhaddon ruled from 681 BCE to 669 BCE. It is not known whether Esarhaddon deported people from Samaria and settled other people there. The cylinder of Esarhaddon, however, notes that he conquered Sidon, and Samaria was likely to be involved in rebellion against Assyria, following which a deportation could have taken place. See Fensham, *Ezra–Nehemiah*, 66–67; Younger, *COS*, 4:175–76.

5. The word for trouble, *ûmbalăhîm*, is a *hapax legomenon* from *blh*. The suggested reading *ûmbahălîm* is more common and means "frighten them," but the meaning in this context is not so different since both words express problems caused to the *golah* community's temple building. Ultimately, the main point is that the temple building is now encountering problems. Thus, it makes sense to read as it is: people of the land troubled them, as explained in the next verse (Ezra 4:5).

A brief comment on the structure of the passage is called for here. Ezra 3:1–6:22 is the temple building account and covers the beginning until the completion of the temple. Precursory works of the temple are narrated in Ezra 3—the altar (3:1–6) and the temple foundation (3:7–13), followed by Ezra 4 that begins with the building of the temple proper, but which soon faced obstructive opposition.

Theme and Structure of Ezra 4

The theme of Ezra 4 is the obstruction faced by the *golah* group in their rebuilding project. The chapter begins with the obstruction of the temple building work (Ezra 4:1–3), which consequently led to the halting of the work (Ezra 4:4–5). The theme of obstruction is further elaborated in the passage following Ezra 4:1–5 with other obstructions the *golah* group faced in their rebuilding project, though from a different time period.

Ezra 4:6, 7 refer respectively to kings Ahasuerus (Xerxes) and Artaxerxes, and are about the wall and the city, rather than about the temple proper (Ezra 4:12).[6] Three letters of accusation against the *golah* community are noted in Ezra 4:6–23. One letter was given to king Ahasuerus (Xerxes), another to king Artaxerxes (Ezra 4:7) and a third one also to king Artaxerxes (Ezra 4:8–10). While the letter of 4:7 does not explicitly mention that it is against the *golah* group the context implies it. Perhaps two different letters were given to king Artaxerxes by two groups of people, but to prove or disprove that here is beside the point, the main point being the several obstructions the *golah* group faced. There were many groups of people standing against the *golah* group and their projects to rebuild the temple (Ezra 4:1–5) as well as the city and the wall (Ezra 4:6–23). Following Artaxerxes's reply in Ezra 4:17–22 the *golah* group was prevented from working (Ezra 4:23).

The chapter then concludes in Ezra 4:24 with a similar phrase from Ezra 4:5b, returning to the reign of Darius after narrating events from his successors Ahasuerus (Xerxes) and Artaxerxes. Such a literary technique of returning to the same or similar point after talking about other things is known as "repetitive resumption," and indicates a "self-contained unit inserted in a longer passage."[7] As such, Ezra 4:6–23 may therefore be un-

---

6. The temple had been built and dedicated during Darius's reign (515 BCE), before the reigns of Xerxes (486–465 BCE) and Artaxerxes (465–424 BCE) (Ezra 6:15).

7. Talmon, "Ezra and Nehemiah," 360. As Williamson notes, this technique of an

derstood as a "parenthetical" unit between Ezra 4:1–5 and 4:24, which further elaborates on the theme of the obstruction against the *golah* group. That is, even though there is a section (verses 6–23) that talks about a later period and projects different from the preceding passage (verses 1–5) that does not cause problems in understanding the narrative. The structure and theme remain consistent. In fact, it presents more significantly how the "other" people are perpetually adversarial towards the *golah* group. Thus, such structuring serves to validate and characterize the "other" group, who were introduced as "adversaries" (Ezra 4:1), as indeed adversarial to the protagonist *golah* group in the narrative. In short, Ezra 4 is structured with the primary theme of the obstructions the *golah* group was facing while they were fulfilling YHWH's command to build the house of God (Ezra 1:2–3). The "other" people, who were not part of the *golah* group, were obstructing their work. While having one running theme, the narrative utilizes two languages—Hebrew and Aramaic.

Brief Note on the Bilingualism of Ezra 4

Ezra 4 switches to Aramaic language from verse 8 and continues until 6:18, but this switch in language does not cause inconsistency in the theme or structure. Not only the documents (Ezra 4:11b–16) but the communications ("narrative seams" [Ezra 4:8–11a, 17a, 23–24]) are also in Aramaic. So, beyond the purpose of quoting documents in their original languages, another purpose for utilizing bilingualism in a narrative, as argued by Bill Arnold, may be at work here.[8] As Arnold argues, a congruent theme, in this case opposition faced by the *golah*, could be one factor for the retention of Aramaic even after quoting the Aramaic documents. For instance, the prophecy of Haggai and Zechariah to resume building inspite of oppositions (Ezra 5:1–2) is still in Aramaic, though they were unlikely to be documented originally in Aramaic. Another factor that may have led to the retention of the Aramaic, Arnold argues, is a shift in "point of view" of the narrator.[9] In Ezra 4:6–18, the narrator's point of view shifted to an

---

ancient author would be equivalent to a modern author's use of a parenthesis or footnote to mark the resumption of a narrative flow after inserting some digressionary materials. See Williamson, *Ezra, Nehemiah*, 57.

8. Arnold, "Use of Aramaic," 1–16.

9. This is a literary device which he adopts from Uspensky. See Uspenskiĭ, *Poetics of Composition*, 8–100.

"externalized viewpoint" from an "internal intimacy" in Ezra 1:1–4:5. That is, the author is externalizing himself while describing the events of the Persian kings and the accusations brought towards the inhabitants of Judah and Jerusalem.[10] Then, in Ezra 6:19, after a transitional paragraph in Ezra 6:16–18, the viewpoint changes back to an internal one and the language correspondingly switches to Hebrew.[11] Later, starting in Ezra 7:12, the language switches to Aramaic again for the same reasons as in the case of Ezra 4:8, since the section starts once more with an Achaemenid letter and a shift in the narrator's point of view.

Joshua Berman further expands the theory of "externalized point of view" by arguing that the purpose of the externalized Gentile point of view is to strengthen the central theme of the whole narrative, that is, the God of Israel is the ultimate champion in the rebuilding projects.[12] In fact, the Gentile point of view even became a reminder to the Jews that when they heed the voice of their God, as they did through the prophets (Ezra 5:1–2), they become successful and finally can complete the temple (Ezra 6). Ultimately, by using another language and "external/Gentile view," the narrator illustrates that the *golah* community prospered because of God.

The above discussion thus shows that, while the original composition of the Aramaic section is beyond recovery, the Aramaic section clearly serves to support the central theme of the whole narrative—that YHWH was the central figure behind the rebuilding task in Jerusalem. That is, the use of Aramaic is not only for the purpose of retaining the original language of the documents, but also a literary apparatus for the purpose of characterization.

As a summary, Ezra 4:1–5 and the rest of the chapter records the obstructions that the *golah* group faced in their building works. Yet, Ezra 4 also is not merely a record of information but serves as a characterization of the "other" group—how they were not aligned with the *golah* group and were adversarial and obstructional towards them. Our main interest is in

---

10. The "externalized viewpoint" seen in the Aramaic portion can be detected in the terms the author/narrator now uses which are different from earlier "internalized viewpoint" passages—such as "the Jews who were in Judah and Jerusalem" (Ezra 5:1), as opposed to earlier *golah* (2:1); "children of Israel" (3:1) and "the God of Israel" (5:1), as opposed to YHWH used earlier; "the house of God which is in Jerusalem" (5:2) as opposed to "house/temple of YHWH, God of Israel" earlier (1:3; 4:1). See Arnold, "Use of Aramaic," 6.

11. Arnold, "Use of Aramaic," 7–8.

12. Berman, "Narratological Purpose," 165–91.

The First Encounter of the *Golah* & Their "Adversaries"

the first face-to-face interaction and dialogue of the *golah* group with the "other" in their initial work on the temple, that is, Ezra 4:1–5, so the rest of Ezra 4 will not be discussed in detail except where relevant. In order to study the factor/s behind the unfriendly encounter portrayed in Ezra 4:1–5, the nature of the adversity needs to be understood first.

The Nature of the Adversity

The usage of the term "adversaries" in this passage (Ezra 4:1–5) is confusing since the text itself does not explicitly present a strong picture of hostility. The "other" people simply came to the *golah* group leaders and offered to build together, stating that they too worshipped the *golah* community's God (Ezra 4:2). In fact, this gesture can be seen positively as a generous and friendly offer to help and support the building work. Yet, it could be that the negative term "adversaries" is used in anticipation of the thwarting they will do to the *golah* group's plan once their proposal is denied. It may be noted here that the narrative is primarily about the *golah* group, thereby the account and characterization of the groups also obviously bear the perspective of the *golah*. At any rate, a study of the term in other contexts would be helpful to examine the use of such a strong term in this passage.

The term *ṣar* is used in other contexts mostly to refer to Israel's adversary or enemy. In some contexts, it is used with war such as when an adversary will overrun the land (Amos 3:11); an adversary oppressing Israel (Num 10:9); where the enemy laid hands on Israel (Lam 1:10); where YHWH raised enemies against Israel/Jacob (Isa 9:11); where Israel was handed over to enemies (Ezek 39:23); to refer to enemy of Israel/Judah (Deut 32:27; 33:7); or where the enemy disrupted daily safety of the people (Zech 8:10). It is unlikely that such war language is implied in Ezra 4:1–5, but in all these references the "enemy" is actively seeking to destroy Israel and is even winning at times against Israel. Perhaps this term is used in Ezra 4:1 in anticipation of the destructive plan the "other" group will later develop by thwarting the building work of the *golah* (Ezra 4:4–5). In other contexts, it may be understood as the enemy of an individual, but where the individual is still representative of Israel, and the "enemy" wishes or is working towards bad ends for the people of Israel. For instance, in Esth 7:4–6, Mordecai's enemy Haman tried to destroy him and all Jews, so Haman is the enemy of all Jews; in Ps 3:2 and 2 Sam 24:13, the adversary/ies of David raised up against him, with David as the representative or king of Israel.¹³ Thus the term in these other contexts still carries a strong connotation of hostility between the two parties in question, mostly between YHWH-worshipping Israel and other non-YHWH worshipping nation/s. The "enemy" is against Israelites/Jews and seeks to destroy them.

Again, in Ezra 4:1–5, the reasons for strong hostility are not clearly expressed. Yet, considering the common connotation of the adversaries/enemies destroying Israel or winning over Israel observed in the uses of the term *ṣar* in other contexts, a similarity is observable in Ezra 4:1–5 (and beyond) as well. As the "adversaries" of the *golah* group eventually destroyed the plans of the *golah* community by blocking the temple work (Ezra 4:4–5), a term like "adversaries" might be employed to foreshadow their later action. Another possibility is that the term is used in a generic sense to refer to anyone or all those who wished an ill-fate for and would work to destroy the *golah*. As such, the term for "adversary" is employed in the text as a categorization of the "other" group—that they are vicious and malicious towards Israel. The "other" people in Ezra 4, then, are not simply apart from the *golah* group but stand in opposition to them.¹⁴

The conversation between the so-called "adversaries" and the *golah* leaders in Ezra 4:1–3 provide some hints about the nature of the adversity. The so-called "adversaries" offered to join the *golah* group in the building work by claiming that they worshipped their (the *golah*'s) God. In response, however, the *golah* leaders said that they alone will build the house of their (*golah*'s own) God (Ezra 4:3; cf. 1:3). Grounding their exclusive authority to build the temple on Cyrus's decree creates the impression of a political or legal reason. And indeed, if Cyrus's decree is taken strictly, it can be interpreted as addressed to the *golah* only since it permits YHWH's people from wherever they were to "go up (return) to Jerusalem in Judah and build the house of YHWH, God of Israel" (Ezra 1:3). That is, it implies a return. Yet, even if one emphasizes the legal reason by strictly applying the command of Cyrus, the narrative presents Cyrus as merely an instrument of YHWH to enable temple (worship) service again. The motivation behind Cyrus in issuing this decree came from being roused by YHWH to build the house of God, which he entrusts upon the *golah* (Ezra 1:1–2). Also, those who

---

13. Some other appearances of *ṣar* may be noted here: enemies of Abraham, the father of the nation of Israel (Gen 14:20); enemy of Joshua the leader of Israel (Josh 5:13). In other contexts, it stands for enemies of YHWH and YHWH victorious against enemies (Job 19:11; Ps 78:66; 97:3; Isa 1:24; 26:11; 59:18; 64:1; Jer 46:10; Nahum 1:2; Deut 32:41, 43).

14. Clines, *Ezra, Nehemiah, Esther*, 73.

did return to Jerusalem to fulfill Cyrus's decree were those roused by God (Ezra 1:5). That is, both the command to return and the act of returning originated from YHWH. Therefore, even the legal reason finally comes down to a cultic one. In fact, not only the *golah* group, but the "adversaries" themselves also claimed cult as their qualification to offer participation in the temple building.

In their proposal to join the *golah* group in building the temple the "other" group claimed a cultic similarity with the *golah* as their credentials. They held that because they also have been worshipping their (the *golah's*) God from the time that they were brought there by the king of Assyria they might join them in building the temple (Ezra 4:2). That is, the claim to validate their participation in the temple building is not based on kinship or familial grounds or some political aspect but rather on cultic sameness. The *golah* group leaders did not comment on the validity of such qualifications for building the temple, so it cannot be known exactly whether they accepted or denied the legitimacy of their claim. However, the use of *your* God by the "other" group ("we worship *your* God" [Ezra 4:2]) and *our* God by the *golah* group ("build a house to *our* God" [Ezra 4:3]) offers a hint. It could imply a cultic difference, that is, the "other" people might not be genuinely worshipping YHWH as they could not even claim YHWH as their own God, while the *golah* community confidently claimed so. Instead, they called YHWH the *golah's* God and said that they worshipped this God as well, perhaps in addition to their own god. Thus, while an argument from these two possessive pronouns alone cannot settle all, the text does imply a cultic difference between the two groups.

The second part of the claim of the "adversaries of Judah and Benjamin" states that they had been brought down by Assyrian king Esarhaddon (Ezra 4:2).[15] There is, however, no way to know whether these people who claimed to have been brought down by Esarhaddon were Israelites from the earlier northern kingdom or were foreigners such as Assyrians brought by the Assyrian king to the land of Israel. Their own self-claim of worshipping

---

15. That is, from sometime during Esarhaddon's reign (681–669 BCE). There is no biblical reference to such a settlement by king Esarhaddon except for a similar reference in 2 Kgs 17:24–41, where King Sargon II settled people in Samaria who also eventually began to worship YHWH, though syncretistically with their own gods. Though not attested, the Assyrian king Esarhaddon could also indeed have carried out a similar tradition of bringing people to Israel. Since this work takes a literary approach, it is neither possible nor crucial to solve the riddle of whether the author mistook the name of the king Esarhaddon with Sargon, or was just not interested in historicity.

the God of the *golah* since their arrival implies the latter case. But, as the text does not tell us the exact identity of the "adversaries," nothing can be known for sure. As noted earlier, the narrative is primarily about the *golah* group and is less interested in the "other" group, often leaving no specific information about the "other" group/s. What the text clearly says is that the "adversaries," unlike the *golah* group, have only worshipped YHWH from a certain point of time, making them either proselytes or a mixture of proselytes and Israelites. As such, the "adversaries" could even be a mixture of Israelites and foreigners.

Needless to say, the temple rebuilding took place with the purpose and hope of future temple service. It can then be assumed that participants in the building of the temple would also be participants in the temple worship and services later, at least in some ways.[16] Following that, it could be that the *golah* leaders wished to keep the worship at the temple and any other services for their own group so they were not ready to welcome others. Even if there could have been another motivation for the "other" to join the *golah* in building the temple, it cannot be known, and the only reason highlighted in the text is primarily cultic—worship of YHWH.

The prominent and intended impression of the text is then twofold. First, these "other" people could not even claim ownership of the God they claimed to worship. Secondly, they have worshipped this God only from a certain point of time. That is, they were not originally part of the *golah* group and were only brought into the land by another king at a certain time. In addition, they were not originally YHWH worshippers. As such, even though the "adversaries" tried to claim similarity by stating that they worshipped the same God with the *golah* community, the text shows that they are not the same as the *golah*. Undeniably, the account of the interaction of the "adversaries of Judah and Benjamin" and the *golah* leaders (Ezra 4:1–5) revolves around cult, the worship of YHWH. Therefore, the adversity between the two groups comes down to cultic reasons and differences. In fact, the centrality of cult can also be seen in the narrative following and preceding the event of Ezra 4:1–5.

Centrality of Cult in the Narrative Following Ezra 4:1–5

After narrating the obstruction the *golah* community faced (Ezra 4), the following section begins with the renewed inspiration for their rebuilding

---

16. Clines, *Ezra, Nehemiah, Esther*, 74.

work (Ezra 5:1–2). This inspiration came from nowhere other than the God of Israel, who spoke through the prophets Haggai and Zechariah. As a result of this inspiration and with full support of the prophets of their God, the *golah* group were able to resume their work. Furthermore, even when they faced another obstacle of being questioned about their permission to build the temple God protected them such that they were not halted from their work while awaiting king Darius's decision (Ezra 5:5). Thus, the resumption of the building work as well as the overcoming of the obstruction is credited to YHWH.

Even in the word of an "other," Persian official Tattenai, the God of the *golah* is presented as the "great God" (Ezra 5:8). The *golah* people also identified themselves as the "servants of the God of heaven and earth" (Ezra 5:11) and attributed the destruction of their former temple ultimately to the action of their own God because of their ancestors' disobedience (Ezra 5:12). Thus, the *golah* people are identified as a cultic people of God, whose fate also rested on their obedience or disobedience towards their God. Furthermore, the temple itself is referred to in a worship or cultic sense—that it is a "place for offering sacrifices" (Ezra 6:3). The edict of Cyrus also ordered that the gold and silver vessels of the (former) temple be returned to the house of God (Ezra 6:5), which implies restoration of the temple service. Following the recovery of Cyrus's edict, Darius ordered Tattenai and his colleagues to co-operate with the building and to supply necessities for burnt offerings to the God of heaven. In this way the function of the temple is presented with a focus on worship and cult (Ezra 6:9–10). The text even employs a technical cultic term, "pleasing sacrifice" (Ezra 6:9-10; cf. Exod 29:18; Lev 1:9),[17] clearly highlighting the temple's cultic purpose.

It is also noteworthy that in the report to king Darius, the leaders are simply called "elders of Jews" (Ezra 5:5, 9; 6:7–8, 14). Considering the fate of their building work at the hands of the Persian government, it would have been natural to claim themselves as the individuals authorized or recognized by the Persian government. Instead they called themselves "servants of the God of heaven and earth" (Ezra 5:11). In so doing, they implied that they were simply servants of God, not of Persians. Such a description indicates the intention to highlight the centrality of God/YHWH and their identity as based on being people of God.

---

17. Berman, "Narratological Purpose," 184. Other references include Gen 8:21; Lev 2:12; Num 15:3, 7, 10, 13–14; Ezek 6:13; 16:19.

Rebuilding a Post-exilic Community

At the conclusion of the account of resumption and completion of the temple building work, the credit is given to the God of Israel (Ezra 6:14). Motivation for resuming the building came from the prophesying of the prophets, and the ability to complete the project ultimately came from the God of Israel, who worked through the Persian kings (Ezra 6:14). Thus, as in Ezra 4:1–5, the centrality of God/YHWH and cult is painted all over the narrative following it. The same is to be observed in the narrative preceding it.

Centrality of Cult in the Narrative Preceding Ezra 4:1–5

In the narrative preceding Ezra 4:1–5, the *golah* community is mainly identified using the term "Israel," such as "people of Israel" (Ezra 2:2b) and "sons of Israel" (Ezra 3:1). The usage of such a term indicates that they are portrayed as the contemporary Israel, a continuation of the pre-exilic Israel. It is unlikely that the term "Israel" here would mean the physical pre-exilic kingdom of Israel or referring to the northern kingdom of Israel. Rather, the term "Israel" seems to be used as a literary designation for devotees of YHWH.[18] That is, "Israel" as used in the passage would not stand for a political group or the land itself but rather for the people as a cultic community—devotees of YHWH. For example, the *golah* community obediently responded to YHWH's command through Cyrus to return and build the temple (Ezra 1:2–3). The same vessels from the former temple, which had been taken away by Nebuchadnezzar were now released and brought back to Jerusalem for the new temple (Ezra 1:4–11). The temple would be rebuilt on its original site (Ezra 2:68), emphasizing that it is the legitimate reconstruction of Israel's original temple of YHWH. The *golah* community, on their arrival in Jerusalem, followed Moses's instruction "correctly" to build the altar to offer burnt offerings (Ezra 3:2), erected the altar on its original site (Ezra 3:3), and observed festivals "as is prescribed" (Ezra 3:4). Thus, the *golah* group was "Israel" in that they were devoted and obedient to YHWH in carrying out cultic activities correctly.

The named leaders also reflect the group's allegiance to YHWH. Zerubbabel is mentioned without highlighting his Davidic line or as being

---

18. Na'aman convincingly argues that the use of "Israel" to refer to "political and administrative life" comes later, in the Hasmonaean period, when "Judea gradually expanded to include the territories of the former kingdom of Israel (Na'aman, "Saul, Benjamin," 348). See, Finkelstein, "Saul, Benjamin," 365.

The First Encounter of the *Golah* & Their "Adversaries"

a governor under the Persians (Ezra 3:2, 8; 4:1, 3). This gives the impression of Zerubbabel as a leader commissioned by YHWH, rather than a privileged Davidic descendant or a representative of Persian power.[19] In fact, it is common to list the *golah* people into cultic leaders, lay leaders and lay people in the book of Ezra (Ezra 1:5; 2:68, 70; 3:8; 6:16). Thus, the named leaders here, Zerubbabel and Jeshua, would represent the cultic leadership and the other leaders would represent lay leadership. Such designation of the leaders implies that the community is primarily seen as a cultic-bound community, with true allegiance to YHWH.

In summary, the passage Ezra 4:1–5 presents YHWH and cult as central in the life of the *golah*. Even where other aspect such as legal or political is noted, as in the claim of exclusive authority to build the temple coming from the authorization of Cyrus (Ezra 4:3) the root reason is still given as coming from YHWH. That is, it has a cultic purpose and origin—Cyrus's permission to rebuild the temple also came as a result of being inspired and entrusted so by YHWH (Ezra 1:1–3). In Ezra 4:1–5 while the "other" group tried to present similarity with the *golah* group by claiming worship of the same God, the text shows that they could not, unlike the *golah*, even claim ownership of that God; and that they, unlike the *golah* community, have only worshipped that God from a certain point in time. As such, the rejection and consequently the adversity would have been rooted in the cultic. No other reason is provided by the text.

The narratives preceding and following 4:1–5 also clearly present the centrality of YHWH and cult, and the temple as the cultic center.[20] These preceding and succeeding narratives, however, do not contain much about the "other" people, except when they are needed to push forward the narrative, by aiding in the fulfillment of the *golah* purpose, as with Cyrus and Darius, or by obstructing them, as with the "adversaries." The narrative is clearly about the life of the *golah* community and only secondarily about any "other" group who are seldom described with specific information, which will also be true in the rest of the narrative. Let us now examine whether there was a pre-existing adversity.

---

19. Williamson, *Ezra, Nehemiah*, 32; Klein, *Ezra & Nehemiah*, 691.

20. Some may argue that the motive behind the desire to participate in the temple building could be for political or economic shares. However, those themes are not highlighted in the text.

Prior Adversity Existed?

There is only one reference to the "other" group with a negative association in the book of Ezra before the real encounter in this passage (Ezra 4:1–5). In Ezra 3:3, the *golah* group were afraid of the peoples of the lands (plural) even though the cause of the fear is not provided. And in Ezra 4:4, the people of the land (singular) caused trouble to the *golah* group's building project. One immediate question is whether the "other" in Ezra 3:3 ("peoples of the lands") and in 4:1–5 ("adversaries of Judah and Benjamin" and "people of the land") should be understood as referring to one or a similar group of people. The book of Ezra is primarily about the *golah* group, and as a consequence vague and unspecific identifications and designations are often used for the "other" people, which seem to encompass any non-*golah* people. Thus, even though it is not possible to confirm whether the exact same people were involved in Ezra 3:3 and in Ezra 4:1–5, the "other" groups involved in 3:3 and 4:1–5 could be understood as belonging together in the broad group of "other" who were not part of the *golah*. With the people causing dread in Ezra 3:3 and the people causing troubles in 4:1–5 understood as belonging to the same "other" group, it can be said that an underlying adversity has already developed between the *golah* group and the "other" even before the adversity of Ezra 4:1–5.

John Tracy Thames argues that the term people of the land, particularly in the post-exilic times, does not carry one meaning throughout all appearances and is used by authors either when they have no other means to identify the subject or even when they intend to imply anonymity.[21] Such usage also seems to be at work in the book of Ezra. The author of Ezra does surely name "other" people in some instances, such as officials or indiviuals and nations (kings of Persia, nationalities of workers [Ezra 3:7] or other names and titles [Ezra 4:7–10]). At other times, however, designations such as "adversaries of Judah and Benjamin" and the phrases people/s of the land/s are used without additional information to further specify the subject/s, giving the impression that they are used intentionally vague. The closest one can get is that the phrase people/s of the land/s may mean what the literal meaning implies, that these are the people living in the land.

On the other hand, some scholars identify and differentiate the groups of people involved in these two passages. According to Fried, all biblical

---

21. Thames, "New Discussion," 110–20. For further discussion on people of the land, see Appendix.

authors, including the author of Ezra, use the phrase peoples of the lands (plural, as in Ezra 3:3) to refer to the neighboring non-Israelite foreigners "who dominated Israel from the time of her settlement in Canaan."[22] In contrast, she argues, the phrase people of the land (singular, as in Ezra 4:4) always refers to the landed "aristocracy, the elites who control and administer an area."[23] She also argues that the "adversaries of Judah and Benjamin" (Ezra 4:1) are the same as the people of the land (Ezra 4:4), and they are the Persian satrapal officials since they were in a position to pay bureaucratic officials.[24] Fried's reasoning is that the redactor made a mistake to assume that these Persian officials were descendants of those brought by Assyrian kings (Ezra 4:3, 10). Thus, for Fried, the "other" in Ezra 3:3 and in 4:4 are not the same—while the peoples in the lands in 3:3 are generally foreigners living around Judah, the people in the land in 4:4 are the Persian satrapies, those in power.

In response to Fried, from the current context and the use of different and rather vague terms for "other" people in the book of Ezra, it is difficult to say whether the phrases peoples of the lands (Ezra 3:3) and people of the land (Ezra 4:4) could be specifically identified and differentiated. In addition, it is unlikely that Persian satrapal officials would come claiming that they were brought down by the Assyrian king, that they worshipped the God of the *golah* group and that they desired to build the temple with the *golah* group (Ezra 4:1–2). Fried herself notes that this claim was a mistake of the author/redactor, but it is a very daunting task to confidently claim an ancient author's mistake or knowledge. Thus, while there is no way to prove whether the two phrases in Ezra 3:3 and 4:4 constitute the exact same people, they do fit together in a broad group of the "other," encompassing any or all non-*golah* people. If the "other" in Ezra 3:3 were already in some kind of adversarial relationship with the *golah* community, the next question then is whether that adversarial relation also relates to cult.

Adversity in Ezra 3:3 Based on Cult?

Ezra 3:3 notes that the *golah* group were in fear of the peoples of the lands when they built the altar. The text does not provide the explicit reasons for the *golah*'s dread of the peoples of the lands, yet some hints can be gathered

22. Fried, *Ezra*, 165.
23. Fried, "Because of the Dread," 458; "'am ha'ares in Ezra 4:4," 130.
24. Fried, *Ezra*, 192, 197; "'am ha'ares in Ezra 4:4," 130.

from the context and the connotation of the term for dread elsewhere. From other contexts, when someone dreads another, the person feels danger, insecurity or even threatened.[25] In the context of Ezra 3, the only details about the activity of the *golah* mentioned are that they built an altar "according to the law of Moses" (Ezra 3:2), at its original site (Ezra 3:3), and that they were observing the festival and burnt offerings "as prescribed" (Ezra 3:4). As such, the ways of the newly arrived *golah* people might have been different from those who have been dwelling there. Or, it could even be that the *golah* people seized the existing altar for themselves, disregarding whatever the existing condition might have been.[26] If such actions happened, an expected reaction from the existing inhabitants would be hostility, causing tension and fear on the part of the *golah* people.

In summary, in the only passage prior to Ezra 4:1–5 that narrates the unfriendly relationship between the *golah* and the "other" centers on cult (Ezra 3:1–6). Thus, while the text does not give the explicit reason for the dread of the *golah*, it does portray the implicit cultic difference between the *golah* group and the "other" people. As such, from a literary point of view, the dread between them could have stemmed from differences in cultic activities between the two groups. This finding is similar to the one reached for the passage Ezra 4:1–5. With such an unfriendly relationship between the two groups, it is curious who constitutes these two groups and how they are characterized.

The Characters

There are two characters in this passage (Ezra 4:1–5). On the one hand, there is the protagonist group, the *golah* group, and on the other hand, there is the antagonist "other" group.

---

25. The term for fear, *'êmâ*, is used in some instances to indicate fear or awe of YHWH's power (Exod 15:16; 23:27; Ps 88:16; Deut 32:25; Job 9:34; 13:21). In other instances, the term connotes terror, dread, or insecurity from death or other human beings (Gen 15:12; Ps 55:5; Prov 20:2; Job 33:7; 20:25; Josh 2:9; Isa 33:18).

26. Jeremiah 41:5 also indicates the presence of an altar and sacrificial activities during the exile. Commentators such as Fensham argue for such possibility. See Fensham, *Ezra and Nehemiah*, 59.

The First Encounter of the *Golah* & Their "Adversaries"

The *Golah*

The protagonist group is identified by the terms *golah* community (literally, "sons of the *golah*") (Ezra 4:1) and "the people of Judah" (Ezra 4:4). From the identifying term *golah* it can be said that the protagonist group is constituted by those who went into exile, and the expression "the people of Judah,"[27] connotes those who have returned and now dwell in Judah. There is no mention or acknowledgment of Israelites who were not exiled or any other people residing in Judah. In addition, the identification of the antagonist group as the adversaries of Judah and Benjamin (Ezra 4:1) reflects the protagonist group, the *golah* group, as constituted by the descendants of the tribes of Judah and Benjamin.

The identification of the protagonist *golah* group has been consistent up to this point in the narrative. The terms of identification used until this point have been—people of YHWH (1:3), Judah and Benjamin (Ezra 1:5), the *golah* (Ezra 2:1), those who came from the captivity (Ezra 2:1; 3:8), and Israel (Ezra 2:2b; 3:1). As observable from these identifications, the central character, the *golah* group, is clearly identifiable while the "other" group is ambiguously identified.

The "Other"

The "other" group is identified variously and vaguely by the terms "the adversaries of Judah and Benjamin" (Ezra 4:1) and "the people of the land" (Ezra 4:4). The "adversaries of Judah and Benjamin" is juxtaposed with "the sons of the *golah*" (Ezra 4:1), indicating that they are not part of the *golah* and are adversaries of the tribes of Judah and Benjamin. "The people of the land" is juxtaposed with "the people of Judah," thus indicating that they would be anyone else in the land but not part of "the people of Judah," that is the *golah* group.

From these identifications of the "other" group, it is clear that they are identified and recognized merely with respect to and in terms of their relationship with the central character, the *golah*. Such vague and merely relative identifications of the "other" show that the narrative is not primarily interested in the "other" group but is rather overwhelmingly about the

---

27. "Judah" here apparently standing for the land Judah, or as commonly called "Yehud" in the Persian period, rather than the tribe, particularly being put in juxtaposition with "people of the land."

protagonist *golah* group. Furthermore, with different terms used for the "other" group, there is no way to know if they refer to the same group of people or not. The best way to understand such vague representation is that any or all non-*golah* people who do not align with the ways of the *golah* are treated and grouped together in one broad group of "other."

Such vague identification of the "other" has also been consistent in the narrative up to this point, such as when they are called the "peoples of the lands" (Ezra 3:3). Yet certain "others" are named specifically such as the Persian king Cyrus (Ezra 1:1, 7–8; 3:7) or the Sidonians and the Tyrians (Ezra 3:7), who do not necessarily carry negative connotations. In fact, king Cyrus is the one through whom the return of the *golah* group became possible, thus he is portrayed positively. The Sidonians and Tyrians were also aiding with supplies for the building of the temple, and are as well positive for the *golah*. It can be concluded that the vague identifications of the "other" usually carry negative impressions while the specific identifications such as named officials or nationalities may not always be associated with negative attitudes.

Who Are the "Adversaries of Judah and Benjamin"?

As argued earlier, though different identifying terms are used for the "other" group even within this passage (Ezra 4:1–5), they still can be understood as forming one broad group. Identifying terms such as "adversaries of Judah and Benjamin" (Ezra 4:1) and "people of the land" (Ezra 4:4), as well as "peoples of the lands" (Ezra 3:3) used earlier in the narrative, are all used to refer to those who were not part of the *golah* group. Despite the unspecific nature of the text, scholars have generally identified the antagonistic "other" as one of three groups, particularly in interpreting the phrase, people/s of the land/s (Ezra 3:3; 4:4)—as non-exiled Judeans, Samarians, or a mixture of non-exiled Judeans and Samarians.[28]

Some associate the "other" group with the Samaritans, perhaps because of the self-description of being brought down by king Esarhaddon of Assyria (Ezra 4:2). For example, Zvi Ron, in a short article on Ezra 4 immediately identifies the adversaries as the Samaritans but without any explanation for the claim.[29] Others such as Cogan treats Ezra 4:1–5 as one

---

28. Bedford, *Temple Restoration*, 12–13. See, particularly, n22–24.
29. Ron, "First Confrontation."

of the biblical portrayals of Samaritan origins.[30] Commentators such as Loring Batten and Charles Fensham also immediately identify the "other" group here as the Samaritans.[31] The text, however, simply does not give clear clues for such specific identification with the Samaritans. The mention of Samaria in Ezra 4:10 may also be easily taken as indicating that the Samaritans were the "adversaries" mentioned in Ezra 4:1, but it is premature to identify the "adversaries" with Samaritans or with any specific group of people since the identifications used in the text are vague. Furthermore, Ezra 4:1–5 is about the temple and set in the reign of Cyrus while 4:6–24 (thus 4:10) is rather about the city and wall, set in the reign of Artaxerses. Thus, they may not be equated with the same groups of people. As scholars such as Coggins and Knoppers convincingly argue, there is no evidence that the conflicts in Ezra (or Nehemiah), such as that of Ezra 4:1–5, are about the "Jews–Samaritan schism."[32] Such specific identification with the Samaritans cannot be proven since the text is at best ambiguous.

As noted earlier, even in that self-description it is not clear whether the text refers to Israelite inhabitants from the northern region or non-Israelites that the king had brought from elsewhere to the land. Furthermore, the whole book of Ezra in general is not very interested in the "other" group, let alone in identifying them clearly. It is thus premature to quickly identify the "adversaries" here as Samaritans and for that matter with any specific group of people. There is simply not enough evidence in the text.

Another designation of the "other" people is people of the land (Ezra 4:4). The term "people of the land" is juxtaposed with the "people of Judah," thus implying difference between the protagonist *golah* group and antagonist "other" group, even though they may be living in the same region,

---

30. Cogan, "For We, Like You, Worship," 286–92.

31. Batten, *Critical and Exegetical Commentary*, 126–27; Fensham, *Ezra and Nehemiah*, 65–66.

32. Coggins, *Samaritans and Jews*, 13–18; Knoppers, *Jews and Samaritans*. Furthermore, the Jews–Samaritan schism is a complex phenomenon, and a quick attribution of conflicts between two Yahwist-claiming groups to such a phenomenon is premature. Hjelm also convincingly refutes the arguments that the Jews–Samaritans divergence began early in the eighth century BCE (based on Assyrian deportations and resettlement policies) (2 Kgs 17) or in the fifth century (based on the expulsion of a priest from the Jerusalem temple) (Neh 13), or even later, in the fourth century (based on the advancing of Alexander the Great, Josephus's Antiochus IV story, and Maccabees), leading to a final schism between the two groups of people. He argues that such arguments are biased as they assume the validity of the Jewish stories of the Samaritans, and thus one-sided. See Hjelm, *Samaritans and Early Judaism*, 11.

Judah. These "other" people are described as simply "people of the land," as if they were living in Judah as usurpers. A similar reasoning has been seen earlier in the narrative as well. In the *golah* list of Ezra 2, there are two sections listed with the names of their domicile instead of fathers' names. In the first section there is no question of the genealogy of those listed from the region of Judah and Benjamin (Ezra 2:20–35), but in the other section the Israelite descent of those from Babylon was questioned (Ezra 2:59–60). It appears that there is a correlation between being of/from "Judah" and truly worshipping YHWH and similarly, not being of/from Judah with not truly worshipping YHWH. One possibility is that the "other" people are those who were in the land of Judah when the *golah* arrived and though they might have worshipped YHWH, it was different from the Yahwistic ways of the *golah* group.[33] As such, their lack of Judean heritage, or being designated as not of Judah, could imply insincerity in YHWH worship.

In summary, the "other" people could be any group of people, such as those Israelites/Judeans who were not exiled and remained in the land, or non-Israelites/non-Jews who lived in the land. In fact, with such vague identifications and descriptions, they could even be people from neighboring provinces. Thus, judging from the text, one is left with no evidence for specific identification of the "other" and it is best to understand the "other" group—identified in this passage as the "adversaries of Judah and Benjamin" and the "people of the land"—as broadly referring to any non-*golah*. What is clear, however, is that the interest of the narrative lies primarily on the *golah* group and on their justification as the legitimate heirs of Israel. Any other group/s who are not part of the *golah* group are secondary for the text and are loosely lumped together in a broad "other," non-*golah* group.

---

33. As Rom-Shiloni points out, Ezra (and Nehemiah) is not the only literature narrating the existence of such "adversarial" YHWH-worshipping communities in post-exilic Judah. Other exilic texts—such as Ezekiel—indicate opposing Yahwistic communities (Ezek 11:15–21; 33:23–29). See Rom-Shiloni, "From Ezekiel to Ezra–Nehemiah," 129. Similarly, Japhet also identifies three Yahwistic communities in the land of Israel—the community of "returned exiles" which settled in Judah and Jerusalem (Ezra 2:1; 3:8; 6:21), another group that comprises the inhabitants of Judah who were not exiled and remained in the land, and a third group of the Israelite habitants of northern Israel who remained in Samaria and Galilee after the Assyrian conquest; and two communities outside the land of Israel—the community of Judean exiles which settled in Babylonia and later also in Persia, and the community of Judeans in Egypt. See Japhet, "People and Land," 104.

Conclusion

As the *golah* group re-settled in Jerusalem and finished laying the temple foundation, they began to rebuild the temple. However, they soon faced obstruction from "other" people, identified as their "adversaries" (Ezra 4:1), who proposed to join them in their temple building work. As the *golah* leaders declined the proposal, the "other" people went on to thwart the building work and got it suspended until the reign of Darius (Ezra 4:4–5). From the analysis of the narrative, the passage (Ezra 4:1–5), as generally with the book of Ezra, is primarily interested in the protagonist *golah* group and not with the antagonist "other" who receives no meaningful identification. It can also be observed that the identification of the *golah* as well as the "other" and the interaction of the two groups are concerned primarily with cult in the sense of worship and allegiance to YHWH. As such, the adversarial attitude and relationship between the *golah* and the "other" would also have been grounded on cultic difference.

The *golah* community's negative attitude toward the "other" people could also be partly the result of their own situation. Being "new" back in the land and trying to settle themselves, naturally they would have wished to be cautious and to do things "right" so as to establish themselves. Later in the narrative, it will be seen that as the *golah* community became more established, they could welcome "other" people who meet the standards of *golah* community membership, as we shall see in the next chapter.

3

"Other" People Join the Passover Celebration (Ezra 6:19–22)

THE *GOLAH* COMMUNITY CELEBRATED their first Passover after the temple was rebuilt and dedicated (Ezra 6:15–18). The Passover account (Ezra 6:19–21) opens with the statement that the *golah* community (literally, "sons of the *golah*") celebrated the Passover (6:19). After noting the purified status of the priests and Levites (6:20) the participants of the Passover are listed: "the Israelites who had returned from the exile" and "all those who had separated themselves from the uncleanness of the nations of the land" (6:21). These participants of the Passover participated in the worship of YHWH, the God of Israel (6:21). The Passover account then concludes with the statement that it was because YHWH had inclined the hearts of the foreign king to support the building of the house of God that they were able to joyfully celebrate (6:22). The challenging question in this Passover account is who might be referred to by the phrase "all those who had separated themselves from the uncleanness of the nations of the land." Are "other" people, that is, non-*golah* people, allowed to join the Passover celebration? Does the *golah* community, who had previously appeared to be closed towards the "other" in the narrative, now welcome and accept "other" people into their community? If that is the case, what might be the criteria to accept "other" people? Or, as some scholars propose, is this passage simply another exclusive account of the *golah* community themselves, with no inclusion of the "other" people?

A literary analysis of the passage will reveal that the *golah* community is celebrating the Passover along with "other," non-*golah* people. That is,

"Other" People Join the Passover Celebration

some people who had earlier not been a part of the *golah* group have joined them in the Passover to seek YHWH. These people, however, are not random people but those who had kept themselves apart from the "uncleanness of the nations" to worship YHWH. The common identity of all the participants of the Passover would then be worshipping YHWH, the God of Israel (Ezra 6:21), which is also the overriding theme of the book of Ezra.

The Event (Ezra 6:19–22)

> [6:19] On the fourteenth (day) of the first month, the *golah* community celebrated the Passover. [6:20] For both the priests and the Levites have purified themselves, all of them are pure. And they[1] slaughtered the Passover for all the *golah* community, for their brothers the priests, and for themselves. [6:21] The Israelites ate—those who had returned from the exile and all those who had separated themselves from the uncleanness of the nations of the land to (join) them, to worship YHWH, God of Israel. [6:22] And they celebrated the festival of Unleavened Bread for seven days with joy, for YHWH had made them joyous and had turned the heart of the king of Assyria to them to strengthen them in their work of the house of God, the God of Israel. (Ezra 6:19–22)

The Passover celebration and the Feast of Unleavened Bread took place after the account of the completion and dedication of the temple (Ezra 4:1–6:18), where Levites and priests were also re-installed for temple services (Ezra 6:16–18). The Passover celebration followed the re-installation of temple cultic worship.

The ability to celebrate joyously is credited to YHWH, who inclined even the heart of the king of Assyria to support the *golah* community in their rebuilding of the house of God (Ezra 6:22). "Persia" is expected instead of "Assyria" here, since it is the Persian kings, not Assyrian, under whom the rebuilding of the temple took place (Ezra 1:1; 4:5; 6:1, 15). However, the reference to "Assyria" may not be taken as too problematic. It could simply have been a scribal error. Or, it could also be that "Assyria" is used as a stereotypical description of foreign rulers and their suffering under foreign kings since the days of the Assyrian kings (as in Neh 9:32).[2] Whatever the

---

1. "They" here would refer to the closest subject, the Levites. That is, the Levites slaughtered the Passover meal for all the *golah* people, the priests as well as for themselves.
2. Williamson, *Ezra, Nehemiah*, 85.

case, the appearance of "Assyria" here does not nullify the purpose of the verse—that YHWH God, none other, is behind the possible joyous celebration following the dedication of the rebuilt temple. Because YHWH turned the heart of a foreign king to favor the *golah* community in their work on the temple, they were now able to complete it and celebrate joyously. The book of Ezra's overriding theme that YHWH is the central figure behind the life and success of the *golah* community is seen here again.

We shall now analyze the Passover celebration account to examine what it reveals about its participants and the membership boundary in the *golah* community.

The Passover Participants

The Passover celebration highlights two important characteristics of the Passover participants. First, it highlights that purity is necessary to celebrate the Passover. The term for pure, *ṭāhôr*, in reference to cultic personnel (priests and Levites) would mean to be ritually or ceremonially clean and fit.[3] Ezra 6:19–20 states that the *golah* community celebrated the Passover *for* the priests and Levites had purified themselves; that is, they were now fit for Passover preparation.[4] The "purity" or fitness of the lay members of the community for Passover is also noted in the next verse, Ezra 6:21. Besides the Israelites who had returned from the exile (6:21a), there is another group of lay participants identified as *all those who had separated themselves from the uncleanness of the nations of the land* (6:21b). Thus, the cultic officials as well as the lay people are all pure and fit for the Passover celebration. Another important characteristic observable in the Passover account is the purpose of participation. Ezra 6:21 states that the participants partook of the Passover in order to worship YHWH, the God of Israel. This purpose of Passover participation to worship YHWH also points, again, to the centrality of YHWH in the life of the *golah* community.

These two characteristics of the Passover—purity and worship of YHWH—imply that the Passover was a cultic ceremony. This Passover

---

3. Someone who is not pure could not offer the Passover sacrifice. As seen in Num 9:6–11, those who are not pure have to wait a month until they can offer the Passover sacrifice. Also, the Passover had to be held in the second month because there were not enough priests who had purified themselves (2 Chr 30:3). See Lev 7:19; 13:13, 17, 37, 39–41; Num 9:13; 18:11, 13; 19:9, 18–19; 1 Sam 20:26; 2 Chr 30:17.

4. Again, cf. 2 Chr 30, where the people had to wait until the next month to keep the Passover because there were not enough cultic officials (priests) who purified themselves.

following the completion of the temple is then a re-inauguration of the cult of YHWH worship, and thus also a re-inauguration of a YHWH worshipping community. The question is who might the participants be.

Besides the cultic personnel (priests and Levites), two lay participants are noted to partake in the Passover meal (Ezra 6:21). The first group of participants is reported as "those who had returned from the exile," which self-identifies as the *golah* people and thus raises no questions. The second group of participants is described as "all those who had separated themselves from the uncleanness of the nations of the land." This second group of participants raises questions about who they might be. If they are non-*golah* people, the Passover becomes a rare occasion in the book of Ezra when "other" people are perceived as not only non-threatening but as welcomed. If they are *golah* people, then the Passover account becomes another exclusivist event as in other parts of the narrative.

In other parts of the narrative, "other" people are often portrayed negatively and even as adversarial. For instance, at the erection of the altar, the *golah* people are said to be in dread of the "other" people (Ezra 3:3). At the commencement of the re-building of the temple, the "other" people are introduced as "adversaries" and were denied participation in the temple building work (Ezra 4:1–3), who then later became inhibitors of the temple building work of the *golah* (Ezra 4:4–5). Later, in Ezra 9–10, the "other" people are said to have abominations and thus to be kept apart from (9:1), and any "other" (foreign) wives whom the *golah* men had married were to be sent away (10:3). Thus, the *golah* community in other parts of the narrative is seen to be very exclusive towards "others." As such, it is curious who the second group of Passover participants are—whether it is still only the *golah* people who participated, or if non-*golah* people are included.

Were "Other" People Included in the Passover?

Matthew Thiessen argues for interpreting the second group of participants as referring to the *golah* group themselves. For Thiessen, the second clause of Ezra 6:21, "all those who had separated themselves from the uncleanness of the nations of the land" is merely an expansion of the first clause, "those who had returned from the exile." Arguing grammatically and from the overall exclusive theme of Ezra, Thiessen claims that this verse is simply a description of the *golah* group themselves. He argues that the conjunction *wĕ* (Ezra 6:21) ought to be translated as a *waw explicativum*: "that is" rather than "and."[5] So, the verse will read: "And all the sons of Israel who had returned from exile, *that is*, those who had separated themselves from the impurity of the nations of the land to them to seek YHWH God of Israel, ate."[6] In this translation, the conjunction really functions as a modifier of the former phrase rather than a conjunction connecting the two phrases. As such, the phrase does not introduce another group of people but only describes the characteristics of the exile returnees as those who separated themselves from the uncleanness of the nations. He argues that the overwhelming theme of exclusion in Ezra–Nehemiah calls for such an interpretation.

While Thiessen's argument is not impossible grammatically, there is not enough evidence to compel this interpretation. The exclusivist nature of the whole narrative does not need to make this event exclusivist too and only about the *golah* community.[7] In fact, this passage does not present a sudden or random inclusiveness but openness with condition/s. It is only those who had met the expectation of having separated from uncleanness of the nations. Furthermore, while it is not impossible to translate *wĕ* as a modifier or with an explanatory function "that is," as Thiessen also admits, that grammatical rule itself is not reason enough to translate it that way in this passage. In many cases of *waw explicativum*, the context is clear and even seems to demand such translation of *waw* into English since the words or clauses before and after the *waw* are clearly the same thing, such as: 2 Sam 14:5 ("Alas, I am a widow, *that is*, my husband died"); Isa 44:1 ("And now, listen, O Jacob my servant, *that is*, Israel, whom I have chosen"); 1 Sam 17:40 ("He put them in his shepherd's bag, *that is*, in the pouch"); Josh 2:1 ("Go to the land, *that is*, Jericho"); Ezra 6:9 ("Whatever is needed, *that is*, young bulls, rams, or sheep"). In Ezra 6:21, however, the context is

---

5. *Waw explicatum*, though not very common, is one of the functions of *waw*. See Thiessen, "Function of a Conjunction," 63–79.

6. Thiessen, "Function of a Conjunction," 73.

7. For Thiessen, exclusivity towards "others" is based on genealogy, which should drive the translation and interpretation of this verse (Ezra 6:21) (Thiessen, "Function of a Conjunction," 77–79). Yet, while exclusivity indeed is clearly seen in the narrative, from the language of the text, it is less clear that it is based only on genealogy, though an important one (for instance, the list of Ezra 2). The exclusivity theme of the narrative seem to be based more on cultic worship of YHWH. The motivation behind the rebuilding of the temple as well as the motivation behind the *golah* people's return to fulfill the temple work, which are the main objectives of Ezra 1–6, are all credited to YHWH and surround the cult of YHWH (Ezra 1:1–5; 3:2, 10; 5:1–2; 6:14, 22).

not clear. So, where the context is not clear, it is necessary to examine the context closely if *waw explicativum* is really demanded.

Thiessen further argues that the three groups of people in Ezra 6:20 for whom the Passover lamb was slaughtered—priests, Levites, and returnees to the land—should match the list in Ezra 6:21. Therefore, in Thiessen's judgment, Ezra 6:21 could not mention a new group of people not already mentioned in Ezra 6:20.[8] As such, since the only group mentioned in Ezra 6:20 is the *golah* group, Ezra 6:21 would also only be about the *golah* group themselves, including the latter part of the verse.

In response to Theissen's argument, there is no compelling reason why the two lists or verses should match exactly. If we look closely at these two verses, it can be seen that they have different emphases. For example, in Ezra 6:20, which actually continues the sense from the previous verse (Ezra 6:19), the emphasis is on the purity of the priests and the Levites, that is, the fitness of cultic officials to prepare the Passover. In Ezra 6:21, however, the emphasis is on the lay people who are partaking of the Passover meal and the purpose of their partaking—to worship YHWH. The term for worship, *dāraš*, is the same as the term used in Ezra 4:2 by the "other" people in their claim to worship the same God as the *golah*. Thus, it has already been seen in the narrative that non-*golah* people claimed to or wished to worship the God of the *golah*. This implies that though rare, it is not impossible that "other" non-*golah* people would come to worship YHWH and would meet the requirement of being separated from "uncleanness." Therefore, it is not necessary to restrict the description of being "clean" to the *golah* group alone.

Even if we were to agree with Thiessen's point that the two lists should match, it still does not seem that only the *golah* group is under consideration. In verses 19–20, the term used for the lay people is "sons of *golah*," while in verse 21 the term used is "sons of Israel," followed by the phrase "those who had returned from the exile," and the second is "all those who had separated themselves from the uncleanness of the nations of the land." It is possible that the identification of the lay *golah* community in the first verse (Ezra 6:20) is now detailed in the next verse (Ezra 6:21) as constituted by "Israelites who had returned from the exile" as well as "those who had separated from the uncleanness of the nations of the land"—that is, those who had not been associated with the *golah* community but were now part of the community as having been separated from "uncleanness." The *golah*

---

8. Thiessen, "Function of a Conjunction," 74–75.

community is now constituted of those who had been in exile ("Israelites who had been in exile") and those who joined them by separating themselves from uncleanness. In short, the two lists of Ezra 6:20 and 6:21 do not have to correspond to the same group since the two verses have different emphases.

Thus, from the text, there is no compelling reason why it has to be only in reference to the *golah* people, those who had been in exile. In addition, in other places where the "sons of the *golah*" are mentioned, there is no accompanying description of them being separated from uncleanness, and it is implied that they are already clean, eligible members of the community (Ezra 4:1; 6:16, 19–20). Apparently, there is no need to explain the existing members as they are those who would already have had separated themselves from uncleanness. If the second group of people in Ezra 6:21 who participated in the Passover were not only *golah* people, what remains unclear is whether these people would be non-exiled Jews/Judeans or real foreigners.

Specific identifications seem less important for the narrative than the characteristics of these people—that they had separated themselves from uncleanness and that they are clean now (Ezra 6:21). As such, it could include anyone, non-exiled Jews or non-Jews, as long as they meet that expectation. Furthermore, in the book of Ezra, being primarily about the protagonist *golah* group, all "other" people tend to be lumped together into a large group comprised of any non-*golah* people, whether non-exiled Jews or non-Jews.

Some scholars also reason that the Passover in Ezra 6:19–21 incorporated "other" people. Fleishman thinks that non-exiled Jews participated, because, he argues, the term "children of Israel" is normally used to "emphasize the religious-national restoration" as seen at three important events: during the construction of the Temple (Ezra 3:1), at the Temple inauguration ceremony (Ezra 6:16) and at the Temple dedication (Ezra 6:21).[9] However, he also does not completely rule out the possibility of non-Jew participants: "returned exiles, together with Judeans and Israelites who had not been exiled, and possibly converts."[10]

Williamson thinks that it must be non-Jews who joined the *golah* group in the Passover, because in this period, Judaism was evolving as a religious community and developing feelings of threats of defilement

---

9. Fleishman, "Echo of Optimism," 20.
10. Fleishman, "Echo of Optimism," 20.

"Other" People Join the Passover Celebration

from those who were "outsiders" even though they might be living close to or among them.[11] Thus, there must be some proselytes who joined the Passover wholeheartedly, because "in the outlook of this writer's circle, the recognition of legitimate Jews who nevertheless stood in a different tradition from their own was generally denied."[12] As Williamson argues, there is no reason to deny that a non-Jew who joined wholeheartedly would have been welcomed to the Passover. Yet, according to that same reasoning, it is questionable why non-exiled Jews could not be included as well if they have met the criterion of separating themselves from uncleanness and join the exile returnees in the Passover. With the text itself not explicitly pointing to a specific identity of who is meant by the phrase, it makes the most sense that it could have included non-Jews as well as non-exiled Jews.

Blenkinsopp also suggests that the phrase must be referring to some local populations, including some from Samaria, who were willing to accept the cult of YHWH alone and joined the celebration.[13] According to Blenkinsopp, the openness in this passage can be understood against the backdrop of other parallel events such as the invitation and participation of northerners in Hezekiah's Passover (2 Chr 30:18–19; cf. Isa 56:1–8). Klein also interprets this verse as an incorporation of Gentiles who had become proselytes, particularly from the use of the phrase "nations of the land," which is used only here instead of the more common phrase "peoples of the land."[14] For Klein, "nations" seems to favor the Gentiles interpretation more. While it is difficult to make concrete distinctions between the phrases "nations of the land" and "peoples of the land" because terms and phrases for "other" people tend to be used in a general sense in the book of Ezra, this passage does seem to imply inclusion of non-Jews in the Passover. Indeed, as Klein also notes, it is not unusual that others can be allowed in the Passover if they meet the criteria (for instance, circumcision in the Pentateuchal law [Exod 12:43–49; Num 9:14]). Also, as Blenkinsopp argues, inclusion in the Passover could imply inclusion into their community. It is not impossible that the *golah* group could be open to other people if they were willing to worship YHWH as they did.

11. Williamson, *Ezra, Nehemiah*, 85.

12. Williamson, *Ezra, Nehemiah*, 85.

13. Blenkinsopp, *Ezra–Nehemiah*, 133. Similarly, Myers views that non-Jews who met the regulations imposed on them were being accepted as proselytes, though he does not lay out what those imposed regulations might be. See Myers, *Ezra–Nehemiah*, 54.

14. Klein, *Ezra & Nehemiah*, 713.

Fried goes as far to identify these "other" people who joined the Passover to be some foreign soldiers and Persian officers who were stationed in Judah and Jerusalem.[15] For Fried, some of these foreign soldiers and officers might have joined the Jerusalem cult. While such possibilities could not be completely ruled out, there is not enough evidence that can be drawn from this isolated passage, nor historical evidence, that Persian officials have joined the Yahwistic cult. The verse itself tells us that the expectation of the YHWH cult of the *golah* community demands exclusive commitment to this God and the leaving of any other gods or lifestyles—"separating from uncleanness of the nations of the land" (Ezra 6:21; also 9:1; 10:2, 11). Furthermore, and without a precedent, it is unlikely that they would be so taken by the cult of YHWH to the point of leaving their own cults and exclusively following YHWH. More significantly, the text provides no further information about these participants. There is simply not enough evidence to narrow it down to a specific, single group of people. Thus, as the text does not allow specific identification, "other" people could include both non-Jews and non-exiled Jews who have met the "criterion," would have participated in the Passover.

A phrase similar to that of Ezra 6:21 appears in Neh 10:29, which will be briefly examined here. Nehemiah 10:29 states: "And all who separated themselves from the peoples of the lands to (follow) the Teaching of God." These groups of people and their families have signed the pledge, along with cultic personnel, heads of the people (Neh 10:1–28) and the rest of the people, the priests and other temple workers (10:29) to follow the Teaching of God given through Moses and to observe carefully all the commandments of YHWH (10:30). This phrase can be understood to indicate that others, non-Israelites, were joining in the renewed Nehemiah community.[16] While Nehemiah (or Ezra–Nehemiah) is generally exclusivist towards "other" people, the fact that they are not randomly admitted but with a specific condition makes it plausible. That is, the "other" people themselves made the claim to follow the teaching and commandments of YHWH. As they were willing to meet the requirement/s of the community, there is no strong reason to doubt that they would have been allowed.

---

15. Fried, *Ezra*, 286.

16. For one who argues that this simply is an explanation of the Jews themselves and no other people, see Thiessen, "Function of a Conjunction," 78. For those who see it as inclusion of "others," see Blenkinsopp (*Ezra–Nehemiah*, 314); Clines (*Ezra, Nehemiah, Esther*, 204–5).

"Other" People Join the Passover Celebration

Now, one may try to compare Neh 10:29–30 with a similar situation seen in Neh 9:2 ("All the Israelites separated themselves from foreigners") to argue for an interpretation of the Israelites/Jews as the only subjects. However, Neh 9:2 clearly states that those who separate themselves from "foreigners" are "Israelites" (literally, "seed of Israel"), while in 10:29 it is simply "all those." It is possible that where the text is vague it is implying non-Israelites, or at least it includes non-exiled Israelites and non-Israelites. Also, as Blenkinsopp notes, this passage can be one of many allusions to proselytism in the early Second Temple period.[17] In sum, while Ezra and Nehemiah are generally exclusive narratives towards "other" people, it can be seen that there are exceptions, particularly when the "others" seem to willingly meet the requirements set by the *golah*/Jewish community. It is not random openness to any "other" people.

Now, if "other" people, including non-exiled Jews and non-Jews, participated in the Passover (Ezra 6:19–21), the question is what such participation means. Would participation in the Passover imply membership in the community as well?

Meaning of Passover and Non-Israelite Participation

While one Passover event may not be identical to another Passover celebration in the Hebrew Bible, some inferences can be drawn on the theme and purpose of Passover to help understand better the Passover in Ezra 6:19–22.

The first biblical Passover account is in Exod 12, where the Passover was celebrated in Egypt.[18] The Israelites were instructed to put the blood of a slaughtered lamb on their doorposts so that the "destroyer" would not kill

---

17. Blenkinsopp, *Ezra-Nehemiah*, 314.

18. The Passover account in Exod 12 is complicated owing to the presence of redundant duplicates (Exod 12:1–13; 12:21–27), with the account of the Feast of Unleavened Bread in between (Exod 12:15–20). The first account of the Passover (12:1–13) is generally assigned to Priestly hand (P), and the latter account (12:21–27) to Yahwistic hand (J) or Yahwist and Elohist combined (JE), though scholars may differ in slight details. See Segal, *Hebrew Passover*, 51–54; Childs, *Book of Exodus*, 184–86; Propp, *Exodus 1–18*, 373–80. However, despite complications in the source assignments and the slight discrepancies between the doublet, the main points of the Passover account/s run parallel—that those who obey the Passover instruction would be protected from being "destroyed." Thus the Passover becomes a marker of who are/would be the Israelites or who could not be part of the community. In that sense, it is related to the Passover account of Ezra 6:19–22, on how the Passover participation could become a defining event for community membership.

Rebuilding a Post-exilic Community

the first born of that house (Exod 12:7, 21–23, 29). As such, the Passover in Exod 12 serves as a differentiating event between the Israelites and non-Israelites. The instruction for future Passover celebrations lists two groups of non-Israelites who are permitted to eat of the Passover meal—a bought slave and a sojourner dwelling with them, but with the condition that they are circumcised (Exod 12:44, 48). The instruction further states that the circumcised sojourner will not only be admitted to offer the Passover but should also be considered equal to an Israelite (Exod 12:48–49). Thus, the stipulation of the Passover of Exod 12 identifies who is and who can be part of the community. By meeting the expected criterion/a, Israelites or non-Israelite sojourners could participate in the Passover and thereby become eligible members of the community. In a similar manner, it can be interpreted that those "other" people who participated in the Passover celebration in Ezra 6:19–21 became part of the *golah* community since they met the expected criterion of separating themselves from uncleanness.

Another Passover celebration is in Num 9:1–14, which took place in Sinai. Two important points in regard to participation in this Passover can be observed. First, those who participate should be clean. Anyone who was not clean or those who were away on a long journey have to wait until the next month to offer a Passover offering (Num 9:6–11). Thus, ritual purity was required. Secondly, a non-Israelite who resided with them was permitted to offer a Passover sacrifice, according to the rules of the Passover, just like the Israelites themselves (Num 9:14). Thus, following the rules and expectations was important. The instruction further states that there should be one law for the Israelites and non-Israelite sojourners (Num 9:14). The Sinai Passover also highlights another important purpose of the Passover. Someone (presumably an Israelite) who was clean and not journeying but did not offer a Passover offering should be cut off from the community (Num 9:13). Thus, participation in the Passover is critical for being a part of the community. In a similar manner, while the criteria in the Passover of Num 9 and in Ezra 6:19–22 may not be exactly the same, meeting the criterion/a would be vital for participation in the Passover, and thereby for membership in the community. As such, the "other" people who have met the criterion and participated in the Passover would be accepted and included in the community.

Joshua 5:10–12 records the Passover celebration in Canaan. While there is no detailed description of the celebration, it is mentioned that before the Passover was celebrated all the men were circumcised (Josh 5:2, 7).

"Other" People Join the Passover Celebration

As such, the participants were fit for the Passover. In a similar manner, the participants of the Passover in Ezra 6:19–21 were "pure" and fit.

In 2 Kgs 23:21–23, the Passover is a part of king Josiah's cultic reform (cf. 2 Chr 35). Even though no details of the Passover are recorded, as part of the cultic reform, it marked a new beginning of the cultic life of the people, a turning away from idolatry and other abominations and a following of the teachings of Moses correctly (2 Kgs 23:24–25). In a similar manner, the Passover of Ezra 6:19–22 could be seen as the inauguration of a "new" cultic community with members made up of those who met the criterion of separating oneself from uncleanness.

Finally, the Passover celebration under king Hezekiah had to wait until the second month, instead of the first month, because there were not enough clean priests (2 Chr 30:3). All Israelites from Judah and the northern region were invited to the Passover as well as to return to YHWH and leave the stiff-necked lifestyles of their forefathers (2 Chr 30:4–9). The temple was also cleared of idolatrous materials and the people offered the Passover sacrifice (2 Chr 30:13–15), while the priests and Levites acted according to the teachings of Moses (2 Chr 30:16). Even though there were some people who partook of the Passover meal even without being sanctified, king Hezekiah prayed for them and they were healed and atoned for by YHWH as they set their minds on worshipping YHWH (2 Chr 30:18–20). Thus, the Passover under Hezekiah emphasizes the participation of all Israel, cultic purity and worship of YHWH.

The Passover in Ezra 6:19–22, like the other Passover celebrations in the Hebrew Bible, is an important event in the *golah* community as it highlights the criterion/a of worshipping members of the YHWH cult. Similar to the Passovers under kings Josiah (2 Kgs 23) and Hezekiah (2 Chr 30), the Passover in Ezra 6:19–22, celebrated after the dedication of the newly completed second temple, marks a new beginning for the *golah* community. It inaugurated a renewed beginning of YHWH worship for the *golah* community, as in the case of Hezekiah's Passover (2 Chr 30), and thus inaugurated a new era of Yahweh worship.[19] As a restoration of the cultic worship of YHWH, the Passover of the *golah* community (Ezra 6:19–22) also serves as a marker of membership in the community. Those who willingly worshipped YHWH by meeting the criterion of separating themselves from uncleanness of the nations were accepted into the community even though they may not have been previously a part of the community.

19. Choi, *Traditions at Odds*, 62.

In summary, while all the Passover celebrations that are recorded in the Hebrew Bible have different accessibility rules, a commonality can be observed. All these Passover celebrations signify some kind of new beginning and with the theme of the Passover participation, these texts discuss, at least in part, who can be accepted to the Passover and thus the community. Indeed, the new condition/s do not necessarily have to overthrow the previous ones but rather would re-install them.[20] As such, in the Passover in Ezra 6:19–22 temple worship was re-installed, being held after the completion of the temple and re-establishment of its services and worship of YHWH (Ezra 6:16–18). As in other Passovers, the Ezra Passover defines "other" people who could be a part of the *golah* community: not random "other" people but those who have separated from uncleanness and joined them to worship YHWH.

As seen in the previous section, those non-*golah* people who joined in the Passover celebration of Ezra 6:19–22 were not random non-*golah* people but "only those who exclusively turn to YHWH."[21] The next question then is what the "uncleanness" means.

Uncleanness of the Nations of the Land

The term for uncleanness, *ṭumʾâ* is often understood in terms of apostasy from YHWH, such as idolatry and participation in the cult of other gods.[22] Outside of Ezra 6:21, the term generally stands for actions that are unacceptable to YHWH, mainly idolatry and sexual transgressions, acts which the Israelites are instructed to shun.[23] The term in another form,

20. Prosic, *Development and Symbolism*, 79–82.

21. As Lau argues, a purpose of Passover is the defining of who can be incorporated into the "true Israel." He argues that not only resident aliens were allowed to participate in Passover at other Passover celebrations in the Hebrew Bible (Exod 12:43–49; Num 9:1–14), but in Deuteronomy also, loyalty to the covenant community is prioritized over kinship, thus it is "consistent with Passover observance by assimilated foreigners" (Deut 16:1–8). See Lau, "Gentile Incorporation," 360, 366, 372.

22. Andre, "*ṭumʾâ*," in *TDOT* 5:330–42).

23. Cf. Lev 16:16, 19; Ezek 22:3–15; 24:13; 36:25, 29; 39:24; Num 5:19; Lam 1:9. The "uncleanness," particularly in respect to the context of "uncleanness of the nations" (Ezra 6:21), would be more in the sense of moral impurity rather than ritual impurity since other nations may not necessarily be expected to participate in ceremonies of Israelites. Israelites, or those already members of the community, would, however, be expected to be morally pure at all times and upon that to be ritually pure particularly for ceremonies or festivals. Furthermore, ritual uncleanness is temporary and easily cleansed and based

ṭāmē' (verb), also refers to actions unacceptable to YHWH and thus actions YHWH's people should not follow. For example, Lev 18:6–24 lists sexual transgressions against the generational and gender order of the kin, child sacrifices to Molech, profanation of YHWH's name, and concludes with a statement how the nations have made themselves unclean with such actions (Lev 18:24, 27). As such, the Israelites should not copy the practices of the nations. Rather, they should practice the decrees of YHWH (Lev 18:24, 26, 30). In fact, any Israelites who do such things would be cut off from their people (Lev 18:29); thus, shunning such actions is an important criterion to be a part of the community. The verb form in other occurrences also mainly refers to sexual transgressions and idolatry and that Israel will be punished because of such sinful idolatry (Ezek 14:11; 20:7, 18, 31; 23:7–49).

While the text itself (Ezra 6:21) does not specify what "uncleanness" means, the term in other occurrences reveals it to be actions associated with the nations of the lands, mainly idolatry and sexual immorality. In other words, the phrase "uncleanness of the nations of the land" is primarily referring to apostasy, which entails unacceptable lifestyles such as idol worship or worship of foreign gods and sexual immorality.[24] Such actions are unacceptable for the people of YHWH. To be a part of the *golah* community one has to separate oneself from such uncleanness of the nations of the land.

The phrase "nations of the land" is also ambiguous. Broadly, it would refer to "other" people who were not part of the *golah* group. As the narrative is primarily about the *golah* community, specific identification of "other" people such as the "nations of the land" are often left unspecific, and thus it is impossible to narrow them down to specific identifications. A more important point than their identification is that such "nations of the land" lived unacceptable lifestyles, which should not be lived by the *golah* community. As such, those who wish to be in the *golah* community have to separate themselves from such lifestyles.

---

on unintentional or intentional contact, while moral cleanness seems to be more of a prolonged lifestyle and based on choice. For more discussions on moral and ritual impurities, see Klawans, *Impurity and Sin*, 22–26.

24. Blenkinsopp, *Ezra-Nehemiah*, 132; Klein, *Ezra & Nehemiah*, 713.

Separation from Uncleanness of the Nations of the Land

The term for separation, *bādal*, implies being set apart and being different from what it is separated from. For instance, the term is used in the Creation account for the separation of light and darkness (Gen 1:4). Light and darkness cannot be mixed. The same term is also used to refer to separation between the Holy and the Most Holy, and the iniquities that separate the people from YHWH (Exod 26:33; Isa 59:2), of setting apart Israelites from other people (Lev 20:24, 26; Num 16:9), or the Levi tribe from other tribes (Deut 10:8). Israelites were to live differently from other people and were expected to keep the commands of YHWH. Thus, the word *bādal* has the connotation of being separated as another, separate group, different or in opposition to other group/s.

The criterion of having to separate oneself from uncleanness in Ezra 6:21 would then have the sense of not being like other nations. They were to be different and distinct from other nations of the land who practiced "uncleanness" such as idolatry and sexual immorality. Instead, they were to live differently and be set apart from such "uncleanness of the nations of the land."

Conclusion

The Passover account in Ezra 6:19–22 debates the theme of the participation of foreigners in the Passover, suggesting a "cleanness" as the pivotal criterion. Besides the Israelites who returned from the exile, "all those who had separated themselves from the uncleanness of the nations of the land" participated in the Passover. These people are non-*golah* people and could have included non-exiled Jews and non-Jews who joined them to worship YHWH by meeting the criterion of separating from "uncleanness." The "uncleanness" of the nations of the land is to be understood as lifestyles of the nations, both cultic and ethical realms, such as idolatry and sexual immorality. This criterion of worship of YHWH as the defining factor of *golah* membership is the central theme of the narrative. The temple being completed, the *golah* community would also have felt to have established themselves back in the land, which would make easier for them to be welcoming of "other" people, while still keeping the same standard. The same criterion that allows "other" people into the community in the Passover account will convict the *golah* community of their failure to maintain that

"Other" People Join the Passover Celebration

expectation, resulting even in the sending away of some "other" people they have let into their community, as we shall see in the next chapter.

4

Rebuilding of the *Golah* Community under Ezra (Ezra 9–10)

FOLLOWING THE ACCOUNT OF the temple re-building and its dedication (Ezra 1–6) comes the account of the rebuilding of the *golah* community under the leadership of Ezra (Ezra 7–10). Ezra 7–8 record the preparation and return of some exiles with Ezra to Jerusalem, and Ezra 9–10 record the rebuilding of the community. The account begins with a report to Ezra that some of the *golah* community members have not kept themselves apart from the peoples of the lands (Ezra 9:1) and have taken the daughters of the peoples of the lands as wives for themselves and for their sons, resulting in the mixing of the "holy seed" with the peoples of the lands (Ezra 9:2; 10:2). This act of not keeping themselves apart and marrying other women is understood as unfaithfulness (*ma'al*, Ezra 9:2, 4; 10:2, 6, 10), and to deal with this unfaithfulness a proposal was made to enact a covenant with God and send away the foreign wives and their children (Ezra 10:3).

This strong disapproval of intermarriage with "other" women leading to the dramatic event of sending them away raises the question why the *golah* community would be so against marrying foreign women. Many arguments have been made to explain this passage about the event of dismissing foreign wives. Some of the suggested rationales include political, sociological, economical, ethnicity or religion to be behind the forced dismissal of foreign wives and the stern requirement to be apart from "other" people. Much of the interpretation depends on the perception of the passage in its larger socio-historical and literary context. This interpretation takes a more modest approach. Because of the lack of extra-textual evidence and the unspecific nature of Ezra 9–10, the varied interpretations lead to no consensus. As a consequence, I offer a literary analysis of the text set within the whole context of Ezra to assess the situation.

A narrative analysis of Ezra 9–10, and the whole book of Ezra, reveals that the narrative is primarily and overwhelmingly about the *golah* community and reflects little interest in the "other" people. As such, the *golah* community's view of "other" people and the solution they took in regard to the marriage of foreign women should first be studied from how they viewed of themselves. The *golah* group perceived itself as a "holy seed" (Ezra 9:2) and as a remnant (Ezra 9:8, 13–15), that is, as the ones set apart by and for YHWH to continue Israel into the future. This self-understanding obliged them to maintain that status and compelled them to be apart from "other" people who followed unacceptable and abominable lifestyles.

The Place of Ezra 9–10 in the Larger Narrative

Before analyzing the narrative, a brief comment should be made about the placement of Ezra 9–10. Ezra 9 begins abruptly with the phrase "when this was over" (Ezra 9:1), when some leaders came to Ezra to report the unfaithfulness the *golah* community has committed. The beginning of Ezra 9–10 appears disconnected from the ending of the preceding chapter which narrates the arrival of Ezra with some exiles and the handing over of royal orders to the provincial governors (Ezra 8:36). It is puzzling whether the people had always been aware of the requirement to keep apart from "other" people and not to marry them, that they would come to report about it to Ezra immediately as he arrived. Perhaps some measures taken after Ezra arrived led them to realize their actions as unfaithfulnesss. A pertinent question is then whether the intermarriage account in Ezra 9–10 would come before or after the account of the study of the law under Ezra (Neh 8).

It seems most logical that the realization of intermarriage as an act of unfaithfulness would come after some kind of a study of the law. Blenkinsopp convincingly lays out the fitness of Neh 8 between Ezra 7–8 and 9–10 from considering both the dates and the contents.[1] From the dates, as the

1. Blenkinsopp, *Judaism*, 61. The other proposal is that Neh 8 fits after Ezra 10, thus concluding Ezra Memoir. This arrangement follows the Greek version that puts Neh 8 after Ezra 10. This argument posits that it makes more sense that the author (Chronicler) would like to end his work with a more festive and joyful situation. This view also assumes that Ezra is presenting a new set of law in Neh 8, as such it is not so related with the actions of Ezra 9–10, which also have the law as its central basis. This view does not

returnees led by Ezra arrived in the fifth month (Ezra 7:8-9), it makes sense that they would organize a public reading of the law in the seventh month (Neh 7:73b; 8:2), which would result in the realization of the unfaithfulness they had committed in the ninth month (Ezra 10:9). From the contents, the public reading of the law in Neh 8 can be seen as a fulfillment of the order given to Ezra by Artaxerxes (Ezra 7:25), followed by the implementation of the law which would be the realization that intermarriage was an unfaithfulness and thus needed to be resolved (Ezra 9-10). Thus, in the flow of the narrative, the intermarriage account would come after the public law reading account of Neh 8.

The Event (Ezra 9-10)

Report of the *golah*'s unfaithfulness to Ezra (9:1-15):

[9:1] When these were done, the leaders approached me, saying, "The people of Israel, the priests and the Levites have not kept themselves apart from the peoples of the lands, with their abominations as the Canaanites, the Hittites, the Perizzites, the Jebusites, the Ammonites, the Moabites, the Egyptians and the Amorites.[2] [9:2] For they have taken some of their daughters for themselves and their sons, and the holy seed has mixed itself with the peoples of the lands, and the hand of the leaders and rulers are foremost in this unfaithfulness.

[9:3] When I heard this matter, I tore my garment and my robe. I plucked out some hair from my head and my beard, and I sat desolate. [9:4] And all who trembled at the word of the God of Israel concerning the unfaithfulness of the *golah* were gathered around me. As for me, I sat desolate until the evening sacrifice. [9:5] At the evening sacrifice I rose up from my humiliation, my garment and robe torn. Then I bowed down on my knees and spread out my hands to YHWH my God. [9:6] And I said, "My God, I am ashamed and humiliated to raise my face to you, my God, for our

---

hold strong, as Williamson argues, since the arrangement in 1 Esdras, being a "secondary compilation," should not be taken as the basis. Also it is now commonly viewed that Ezra is not necessarily bringing a new law but that the people have neglected it or perhaps Ezra was just presenting a fresh interpretation. See Williamson, *Ezra, Nehemiah*, 284-85.

2. It is possible to read "Edomites" by following 1 Esdras 8:69 instead of Amorites. Yet, the list of nations is random anyway, not referring to these nations exactly but simply for the purpose of stereotyping, thus, it does no harm to stick with the MT as Amorites.

iniquities have accumulated to our heads and our guilt has grown to the sky. [9:7] From the days of our fathers[3] we have been in great guilt until this day. And in our iniquities we, our kings, our priests have been given into the hands of the kings of the lands, to the sword, to the captivity, to plunder and to the shame of our faces as is now the case. [9:8] But now, for a brief moment, there is favor[4] from YHWH our God to spare us a remnant and to give us a stake[5] in his holy place. Our God brightens our eyes and gives us a little regeneration[6] in our slavery. [9:9] For we are slaves, but in our slavery our God has not abandoned us. He has extended steadfast love before the kings of Persia to give us regeneration to raise the house of our God, to repair its ruins and to give us a wall in Judah and Jerusalem.

[9:10] Now, O our God, what can we say after this, for we have abandoned your commandments [9:11] which you commanded through your servants the prophets, saying, "The land which you are entering to possess is a land unclean with the uncleanness of the peoples of the lands by their abominations. They have filled it from end to end with their impurity. [9:12] So now, do not give

---

3. "The days of our fathers" would be referring to the pre-exilic days. This would also be a literary tool to link the *golah* community to the pre-exilic Israel, thus, being the continuation of the Israel.

4. The term *tĕḥinnâ* in this context is best described by the English word "favor." Despite the sinful situation of the people and deserving complete destruction, they were not only saved from the destruction but were given a favor to be spared as a remnant and a hope ("a brightening of the eyes") to start a new life again ("regenerate") (cf. Josh 11:20; 1 Kgs 8:30, 52; Ps 119:170). The term has been translated in different ways in English— for instance "mercy" (Blenkinsopp, *Ezra-Nehemiah*; Fried, *Ezra*), "grace" (Williamson, *Ezra, Nehemiah*). BDB lists the meaning as "supplication for favor" (Josh 11:20; 1 Kgs 8:30,52; Ps 119:170).

5. There is an editorial suggestion to change the word *yātēd* (stake or peg) into *yeter* (remainder or remnant) as attested in one other Hebrew manuscript. But "a stake or tent peg" is preferable since the term (remnant) could be an emendation or scribal smoothening from the previous appearance of the term in the same verse. Also, the Hebrew consonants *r* and *d* look similar and could easily be mistaken. Thus the more difficult and unexpected reading would be the more original.

6. I translate the word *miḥyâ* as "regeneration" since it has the connotation of a reviving of life in addition to preservation or sustenance. For instance, in Gen 45:5, the term connotes the preservation and thereby regeneration of Jacob's family despite the famine, through Joseph in Egypt to provide food and livelihood. In Judg 6:4; 2 Chr 14:12, the term expresses no sustenance and thus no means of recovery and regeneration left after an attack. The reviving or regeneration of life also fits in the context of Ezra 9:8 and larger narrative since the *golah* community is perceived not just to be spared from total destruction but to continue the life of Israel into the future.

your daughters to their sons and do not take their daughters for your sons. Also, you shall not seek their well-being and prosperity in order that you may be strong and eat the good things of the land and bequeath it to your children to inherit it forever. [9:13] After all that came upon us because of our evil deeds and our great guilt, since you our God have punished us less than our iniquities deserved and have given us a remnant as this, [9:14] shall we break your commandments again and intermarry with the peoples of these abominations? Would you not be angry at us until there is no remnant or survivor at all?

[9:15] O YHWH God of Israel, you are righteous, for we are spared as a remnant as today. Here we are before you with our guilt, for no one can stand before you on this account. (Ezra 9:1–15)

Salient points about the *golah* community seen in this passage will be pointed out briefly. First, the *golah* community is listed as the "people of Israel" (lay people) and the priests and Levites (cultic people),[7] implying that the whole community is guilty of this unfaithfulness (Ezra 9:1). Second, according to the text, the unfaithfulness (*ma'al*) of the *golah* community is in not keeping themselves apart from "other" people (Ezra 9:1). More precisely, the unfaithfulness committed by the *golah* community is in marrying the women of the peoples of the land, which resulted in the mixing of the holy seed with the peoples of the lands (Ezra 9:2; see also 9:4; 10:6). Third, the *golah* community is presented as a continuation of the pre-exilic Israel. They carried the accumulated guilt and were under foreign rulers in exile because of their continued iniquities committed since the days of their forefathers (Ezra 9:6–8, 13). But now, the *golah* community received a favor from God to be spared as a remnant despite their guilt and iniquities since the days of their forefathers (Ezra 9:8). That is, the *golah* community understood itself as the one continuing pre-exilic Israel to carry it forward to the future. Spared and saved as a remnant, the *golah* community would regenerate the life of Israel. Ezra 9:9 continues to express how YHWH was the real actor, allowing favor for the *golah* community in the eyes of the foreign kings so they could rebuild the temple. The *golah* community was also given a wall in Judah and Jerusalem. The term for wall, *gādēr*, stands for a fencing wall or a protective wall (Num 22:24; Isa 5:5; Ps 62:4; 80:13; Ezek

---

7. Such listing is usual in the book of Ezra (Ezra 2:2b, 36, 40, 70; 6:16, 20, 21; 8:15, 29; 10:5, 18, 23, 25).

13:5; 22:30). Thus, the use of this term highlights how they were granted protection, even while under slavery.

The passage also mentions non-*golah* people, using the phrase peoples of the lands. The phrase peoples of the lands (Ezra 9:11) appears to refer to the people who lived in the land before the Israelites conquered it. So it is unclear whether the same phrase in Ezra 9:11 and earlier, in 9:2, where it refers to their contemporaries, are used in different ways. First, it must be noted that this mention is made within the prayer of Ezra quoting commandments.[8] Secondly, in the book of Ezra, all or any non-*golah* people tend to be treated together into one broad "other" group, without further specific identification. Thus, while the peoples of the lands in Ezra 9:1 and in 9:11 are referring to different peoples from different periods of time, they still belong together to the one broad group of "other." The specific identifications are beside the point for the theme of the narrative. Rather, the point of the narrative is that the *golah* people should not to be like these "other" non-*golah* people and should be apart from them. What is common between these two appearances of the phrase (Ezra 9:1; 9:11) is that both peoples have abominations that were not acceptable for the *golah* people. Thus, following the above points, the same phrase in verse 2 and in verse 11 are not necessarily inconsistent and what the text conveys is that the *golah* people were not to be like them, not to follow their abominable lifestyles and be apart from them.

Resolution for the Community's Unfaithfulness (10:1–45)

> [10:1] While Ezra was praying, confessing, weeping and throwing himself in front of the house of God, a very large number of men, women and children from the Israel assembly[9] gathered to him, for the people wept bitterly.

---

8. The quotations, however, do not come from a single text. As Blenkinsopp notes, they could have been composed from several texts, such as: "The land which you are entering to possess" (Deut 7:1); "A land unclean by the uncleanness of the peoples of the lands" (Lev 18:27); "By their abominations" (Deut 18:12; 2 Kgs 16:3); "Which filled from edge to edge" (2 Kgs 10:21; 21:16); "Do not give your daughters" (Deut 7:3); "Do not seek their well being or prosperity" (Deut 23:7); "That you may eat . . . eat the good things of the land" (Deut 6:11); "To your children as an inheritance for ever" (Deut 1:38–39). See Blenkinsopp, *Ezra–Nehemiah*, 185.

9. The use of the term, *qāhāl* (assembly), would indicate that by this time, having rebuilt the temple, the *golah* community would have an organized assembly/congregation

[10:2] Then Shecaniah son of Jehiel from the descendants of Elam responded and said to Ezra, "We have been unfaithful to our God and we have married[10] foreign women from the peoples of the land, but even now there is hope for Israel on this account. [10:3] Now, let us make a covenant with our God to send away all the women and those born from them, according to the advice of my lord and those who tremble at the commandment of our God. Let it be done according to the law. [10:4] Arise! It is your responsibility, and we are with you. Be strong and act!

[10:5] Then, Ezra arose and made the leaders,[11] priests, the Levites and all Israel to swear to do according to this proposal. And they swore. [10:6] And Ezra arose in front of the house of God and he walked to the room of Jonathan son of Eliashib. He went there without eating bread nor drinking water for he was mourning over the unfaithfulness of the *golah*.

[10:7] So they made a proclamation in Judah and Jerusalem to all the *golah* community to assemble in Jerusalem. [10:8] And anyone who does not come within three days according to the counsel of the leaders and elders, will have all his property confiscated. Also, he will be separated from the assembly of the *golah*.

[10:9] So, all the men of Judah and Benjamin assembled in Jerusalem within the three days. It was on the twentieth day of the ninth month. All the people were sitting in the open square of the house of God, shivering on account of the matter as well as from the heavy rain.

[10:10] Then Ezra the priest stood up and said, "You have acted unfaithfully and married foreign women to increase the guilt of Israel. [10:11] Now, make confession to YHWH the God of your fathers and do his will. And keep yourselves apart from the peoples of the land and from the foreign women." [10:12] And all the assembly answered in loud voice, "We shall do according to

---

(cf. Ezra 10:8, 12, 14, where delegated leaders seemed to be in operation). In this specific verse, however, a general, spontaneous gathering of people resulting from the weeping of Ezra and other people around him, seems to be the case.

10. The term for "married" is *yāšab* (Hiphil), which literally means *cause to sit or dwell*. This same term is also used in Ezra 10:10, 17–18.

11. The "leaders" here would be lay leaders, while the Levites and the priests are the cultic leaders.

your word upon us. [10:13] But, the people are many and it is the rainy season, so we cannot remain out here. Moreover, the work is not for a day or two because many of us have transgressed in this matter. [10:14] So, let our leaders stand for the whole assembly and let all who are in our towns who have married foreign women come at appointed times, along with the elders and judges of each town, until the anger of our God is averted from us on this matter."

[10:15] Only Jonathan son of Asahel and Jazeiah son of Tikvah stood against this,[12] and Meshullam and Shabbethai the Levite helped them. [10:16] Thus the *golah* community did so. Then, Ezra the priest and the heads of the families were selected[13] according to each families and each of them by their names. So they sat on the first day of the tenth month to examine the matter. [10:17] By the first day of the first month they finished (dealing) with all the men who married foreign women.

[10:18] And among the descendants of the priest were found who had married foreign women: from the descendants of Jeshua son of Jozadak and his brothers: Maaseiah, Eliazer, Jarib, Gedaliah. [10:19] These pledged to expel their wives. And their guilt offering was a ram of the flock for their guilt. . . .

[10:20–43] [the names of those who had taken foreign women]

[10:44] All these had married foreign women. And some of them (with their) wives had children. (Ezra 10:1–44)[14]

---

12. Some other versions, such as the Greek, read "with me" instead of "against." However, in this context, with the adversative *'ak* at the beginning, reading as "against" is preferable. Furthermore, considering the larger context, it seems that the proposals for the action is generally accepted by many people.

13. Some other versions such as the Greek have "Ezra separated . . . for himself," which solves the possible confusing question here—who is commissioning and who is commissioned. Many modern commentators also follow that smoother version (e.g., Williamson, *Ezra, Nehemiah*, 140; Blenkinsopp, *Ezra-Nehemiah*, 191; Fensham, *Books of Ezra and Nehemiah*, 137). The Masoretic Text version—as it is, "Ezra and the heads of families were selected/commissioned"—is not totally insensible (commentators such as Lisbeth Fried keeps this MT version; see Fried, *Ezra*, 389). It could just be that the author has no intention of pointing out the commissioner.

14. The Hebrew text is corrupted, and what remains literally reads, "And there was among them (masc) women/wives and they (masc) had children." The Greek version has, "And they sent away with their children" (1 Esd 9:36), which probably is a smoothening after considering the larger context of considerations to send them away.

Following the reaction of Ezra to the unfaithfulness of the community, the people also responded with deep concern and they resolved to deal with their unfaithfulness in quite a dramatic way of sending away their foreign wives and their children. As in Ezra 9, where all parts of the community were involved in the unfaithfulness, the whole community now responded to this unfaithfulness: "a very great assembly," which includes "men, women and children," gathered around Ezra (Ezra 10:1). The people expressed deep regret by "weeping bitterly" (Ezra 10:1). Then, a proposal was made to fix their unfaithfulness which would be in obedience with the law (Ezra 10:3b) and following the advice of their leader Ezra and "those who tremble at the command of God" (Ezra 10:3). Thus, the whole *golah* community came together to pledge themselves to God in an attempt to resolve their unfaithfulness of *not having kept themselves apart* from "other" people.

Ezra 10:20–43 list the men involved in marrying foreign women. Compared with the list in Ezra 2, it is a small percentage of the community that have committed this unfaithfulness.[15] Thus, while marriage is strongly disapproved of, number-wise, the issue seems to be a relatively small one.

The ending of chapter 10 is corrupted, which literally reads: "And there were some of them (masc) women and they (masc) had children." So it cannot be known whether the foreign women and their children were actually sent away (Ezra 10:44). In addition, only the priests are attested to make a pledge to send away their foreign women, with no indication whether they actually followed through (Ezra 10:19). In fact, no laymen are recorded to make such a pledge to send away their foreign wives and children. Here the narrative ends, leaving no clue of what happens next with the *golah* community. This verse (Ezra 10:44) as it is can be made sense of by reading it as a statement that some of the *golah* men married foreign women and some even have children. After all, it is the ending statement of the account about the *golah* community intermarriage. No further investigation is possible to see whether foreign wives and children were absent from the community from that moment or might still be part of their community. At any rate, the more important question is what the hostile attitude towards "other" people was based on, not whether the event of sending away of foreign wives and children actually occurred. And an initial step to understand the attitude between the *golah* and the "other" is their identification and their characterization in the narrative.

---

15. Klein, *Ezra & Nehemiah*, 745–46.

The Characters

There are two main characters in Ezra 9–10, namely, the protagonist *golah* group and the antagonist "other" group.

The Protagonist Group

The protagonist group is designated by terms such as "Israel" (Ezra 9:1; 10:1–2, 5), "the *golah*" (Ezra 9:4; 10:6; "sons of the *golah*" [Ezra 10:7, 16]), "remnant" (Ezra 9:8, 13–15), "assembly" ("assembly of the *golah*" [Ezra 10:8]; "the entire assembly" [Ezra 10:12, 14]), "men of Judah and Benjamin" (Ezra 10:9). They are also presented as attentive and willing to obey YHWH ("those who tremble at the command of God" [Ezra 9:4]; "those who tremble at the command of our God" [Ezra 10:3a]; the solution proposed to fix the unfaithfulness will be according to the law [Ezra 10:3b]). From such designations, it can be seen that the protagonist group is constituted by the *golah* community, who understood themselves to be the remnant Israel, spared from total destruction to continue Israel to the future.

In Ezra 9:4, "all those who trembled at the word of God" gathered around Ezra. Blenkinsopp compares this passage with Isa 66:2, 5, the only other place where the term appears, and concludes that this term refers to Ezra's support group, made up of a "prophetic-eschatological group which espoused a rigorist interpretation of the law."[16] The "trembling" would be in a sense of "religiously-inspired terror or awe" (cf. Exod 19:16; 1 Sam 14:15).[17] Thus, for Blenkinsopp, as in Isa 66:5, where those few elect people are pointed out to rejoice in opposition to another group that will be shamed, in Ezra 9–10, this term refers to the support group of Ezra, whose presence is emphasized in opposition to the conspicuous absence of the priests.[18] The term could indeed mean a certain organized, small group of people, as Blenkinsopp argues. Or, it could also simply be a description of all those who gathered around Ezra arbitrarily, implying that those deeply

---

16. Blenkinsopp, *Ezra-Nehemiah*, 178–79.

17. Blenkinsopp argues that this term is used to refer to "the devout in post-destruction prophetic writings (Isa 56:6; 59:19; 60:9; Mal 1:6–7, 11, 14; 2:5; 3:16, 20)" (Blenkinsopp, *Isaiah*, 299–300).

18. Ezra would also be a part of this group, judging from his emotional reaction of the news (Ezra 9:3–5), his asceticism (10:6), penitential prayer (9:6–15), and fasting and mourning (9:4; 10:6). See Blenkinsopp, *Isaiah*, 301.

concerned by the news that their community has committed a serious mistake has gathered around Ezra.

In the book of Ezra specific identifications are seldom made. For instance, the report of the unfaithfulness is brought to Ezra by "leaders," who apparently would be some lay leaders (Ezra 9:1), but no specific identification is provided by the text. Apart from the common listing of the community into priests, Levites (cultic officials) and Israelites (lay), specifications are not emphasized in the text. Furthermore, the verse itself describes that these tremblers at the word of God were concerned about the unfaithfulness of the *golah* community (Ezra 9:4). As such, they would be people who were especially affected by this bad news for their community. As the realization of their mistake would come from the conviction of the word of God, which would cause them to tremble, they would also be in fear or bewildered by what might befall them because of this unfaithfulness. As such, they would have gathered around Ezra looking for advice or counsel in how to respond this (Ezra 9:1; 10:1, 3, 12; cf. Ezra 3:1). The phrase "tremblers at the word of God" in this verse seems to be intended to point generally to all—including any "support group" people zealous for the law, if Ezra had such a group—who gathered around Ezra particularly on account of this unfaithfulness of the *golah* community. There is no compelling reason, *pace* Blenkinsopp, that this phrase has to be restricted to certain selected group of people. Ezra 9–10, as is the whole book of Ezra, emphasizes participation of the whole community (cf. Ezra 9:4; 10:1). This phrase also reaffirms the centrality of the word of God for the *golah* community (cf. Ezra 10:3).

The Antagonist Group

The antagonist group in Ezra 9–10 is designated mainly by the terms peoples of the lands (Ezra 9:1–2, 11), peoples of the land (Ezra 10:2, 11) and foreign women (Ezra 10:2, 10–11, 14, 17–18, 44). There are no further identification for these terms. Some argue that "the peoples of the land" are not really "other" but simply those Jews who did not go into exile, thereby the issue would be inner-Yehudite conflicts,[19] while others argue that there is no evidence of inter-Yehudite conflicts.[20] In response to these two opposing views, the text itself remains vague when in comes to identification and

19. See, for instance, Becking, "On the Identity," 31–43; Williamson, "Welcome Home," 113–23.
20. See for instance, Oded, "Time of Zerubbabel," 265.

description of the "other" people. The text provides no further information to identify the peoples of the land/s genealogically or nationally.

The choice of the term *nokrî* ("foreign," Ezra 10:2, 10–11, 14, 17–18, 44) gives the impression that the women were non-Israelites, as the term usually refers to someone "outside the family," someone not of the people of Israel and coming from a distant land (1 Kgs 11:1; Deut 17:15).[21] It refers to someone belonging to another family, clan, tribe, or nation.[22] It thus seems that these women are not simply non-exiled Jews but real foreigners, that is, non-Israelites. Yet, the term also correlates with the peoples of the land—"foreign women from the peoples of the land" (Ezra 10:2; cf. peoples of the land *and* foreign women [Ezra 10:11]). With no further information to specify the identity of the women, it could be a designation that includes both non-exiled Jews and non-Jews. Considering the larger narrative, what seems more problematic with the *foreign* women is not whether they are real foreigners or non-exiled Jews, but that they did not align with the Yahwistic *golah* community standards. Thus, in the narrative which is primarily about the *golah* community any "other" people who do not belong to the *golah* group are treated together as belonging to a broad "other" group, regardless of whether one is a "real" foreigner or simply a non-exiled Jew.

The one piece of information the text does provide about the "other" people is their enumeration in a list with other people who have abominations *like* those of the Canaanites, Hittites, Perizzites, Jebusites, Ammonites, Moabites, Egyptians, and Amorites (Ezra 9:1, 11). Such a characterization itself does not however specifically identify the "others" because they are simply likened to the actions of some nations of the past. In fact, there is no exact source of these nations appearing together in the Hebrew Bible. The first four and last nations in the list (Canaanites, Hittites, Perizzites, Jebusites, Amorites) could have come from Deut 7:1, nations with whom intermarriage is prohibited for fear of apostasy (Deut 7:3–4).[23] The other two nations (Ammonites and Moabites) could have come from Deut 23:4, and referred to those who should not be admitted into their assembly. Evidently, this listing of nations is random and serves more to stereotype rather than reference specific nations. As such, the antagonist "other" people could be anyone, any group of people other than the *golah* group who lived such

---

21. See Ringgren, "*nokrî*," in *TDOT* 11:425–29).
22. Clines, *Dictionary*, 5:694.
23. Williamson, *Ezra, Nehemiah*, 131.

lifestyles as those stereotyped nations and are unacceptable to the Yahwistic *golah* community, as is the case in earlier parts of the narrative.

In sum, the antagonist "other" people could include anyone—non-exiled Judeans or non-Israelites—who were not part of the protagonist *golah* community and who lived abominable lifestyles unacceptable for a *golah* community member. The vagueness of the text, particularly in regard to the antagonistic, non-*golah*, group is not unusual for the book of Ezra, as seen in preceding chapters.

Interpreting the Passage

Ezra 9–10, which covers the account of the failure of the *golah* community to keep themselves apart and their intermarriage with foreign women have attracted varied interpretations. Such a variety of interpretations might be because of the unprecedented nature of the event and because of the dramatic action the *golah* group attempted to take in sending away all foreign wives and their children. As such, before analyzing the passage or the varied interpretations, the unprecedented nature of the event will be briefly summarized.

Unprecedented Situation

It is noteworthy that the situation itself is unprecedented and unparalleled in the Hebrew Bible, and the text further uses unconventional terms. While intermarriage with non-Israelites is not always viewed positively in the Hebrew Bible (Deut 7:3; Exod 34:16; 1 Kgs 11:1–5), there is no Pentateuchal law that specifically prohibits intermarriage with all foreigners in general. There is a prohibition on intermarriage but it specifically relates to the seven Canaanite nations—the Hittites, Girgashites, Amorites, Canaanites, Perizzites, Hivites, and Jebusites, and the reason behind such prohibition is also given—because they would be led astray by the foreign spouses to worship other gods (Deut 7:1–4; Exod 34:11–16). The intermarriage situation in Ezra 9–10 is unprecedented in that it apparently applies to all foreigners and no clear reason is offered in terms of what the foreign women would do to their Jewish husbands.

Ezra 9–10 also uses unprecedented phrases and logic. The peoples of the land are associated with impurity, *ṭumʾâ*, and abominations, *tôʿēbâ*: "The impurity of the peoples of the land" (Ezra 9:11), which is unattested elsewhere in the Hebrew Bible.[24] Secondly, the terms used for marriage/intermarriage are varied and some are not strictly technical terms. One of the terms used for marriage is *yāšab* (Hiphil), which literally means *to cause to sit or dwell*, and it is used in connection to marriage only in Ezra and Nehemiah (Ezra 10:2, 10, 14, 17, 18; Neh 13:23, 27).[25] As such, one can even interpret the term to imply that a legitimate marriage did not take place but a couple only lived together, or that the men simply "placed" the women in their households.[26] Another term is *nāśā'* (qal) (Ezra 9:2, 12), which literally means *to take, lift, or carry*, though in late Hebrew, this term can mean *take (as wife) in marriage* (Neh 13:25; 2 Chr 11:21; 13:21; 24:3; Ruth 1:4). Still other terms used to refer to intermarriage are *nātan* (qal), which means *to give a (woman) to a man in marriage*, (Ezra 9:12)[27] and *ḥātān* (Hithpael) (Ezra 9:14), which means to *become a son-in-law*.[28] Perhaps varied terms are used, including unconventional ones, because the union was strongly disapproved of.

The proposed solution also carries unclear terms, perhaps because there is no established solution or response if someone breaks the law and marries a foreigner. One of the terms used for the solution is *yāṣ'* (Hiphil, to "put out") (Ezra 10:3, 19), which is not a common term for divorce.[29] Not only the women but also their children were to be sent away. This implies that not only the foreign women were seen as "other" but also their children, even though the fathers were *golah* men. Furthermore, the children of the foreign women are also worded as "those borne to them" (Ezra 10:3), not even "their children," as if they were the products of these women.[30] Thus, while the use of these non-technical terms does not rule out intermarriage as the issue or that divorce is not meant, it is likely that the text does not even want to employ technical terms for marriage as it is strongly

---

24. The term "impurity," which is usually used to refer to ritual impurities in the Torah, is used in Ezra in direct link to non-Israelites. See Harrington, "Intermarriage in Qumran Texts," 254–55.

25. BDB 443.

26. Southwood, "Holy Seed," 190; Japhet, "Expulsion of the Foreign Women," 153.

27. See BDB 678. Also Neh 13:25; Gen 29:19, 26, 28; 34:8–9, 12, 14, 16; Josh 15:16, 17; 1 Sam 25:44.

28. BDB 368. Also in Gen 34:9; 1 Sam 18:21–23, 26–27; 1 Kgs 3:1; 2 Chr 18:1; Deut 7:3; Josh 23:12.

29. The expected term for divorce would be *šālaḥ* or *gāraš* (Gen 21:14). See Yoo, *Ezra and the Second Wilderness*, 188; Japhet, "Expulsion of the Foreign Women," 147, 152.

30. Japhet, "Expulsion of The Foreign Women," 152.

disapproving of these unions. In other words, the unions between *golah* men and "other" women are not upheld as valid marriages.

More importantly, and perhaps because it was an unprecedented situation, not only the text employs unconventional terms, the reason for keeping oneself apart from the "other" people, is also not clear, except that by failing to keep themselves apart the holy seed had been mixed with the peoples of the land/s.[31] It is also not clear how they were to remain separated—should they not mingle socially as well? In the Deuteronomic stipulation not to let some people in the congregation, it states who is not to be admitted—"whose testes are crushed (Deut 23:2) and no Ammomite or Moabite (Deut 23:4). The reason is noted as well—for instance, because the Ammonites or Moabites did not meet them with food and water (Deut 23:5). In Ezra 9–10, however, the reasons are not provided, at least not explicitly.

Different Explanations of the Passage

As noted above, the text is unclear in some ways and while much research has been done and several rationales proposed to explain the intermarriage issue in Ezra 9–10, there is no consensus. A few examples of the varied interpretation of the text will be cited below.

Some see the reason behind the "forced divorce" to be a political one, not cult or orthodoxy of the faith. For instance, Wolfgang Oswald argues that those who investigated the case were civil leaders (Ezra 10:8), and also since the expulsion is said to be from the "assembly of exiles," an institutional body, the actors defined themselves politically as an association of persons.[32] In response to Oswald, while the term for leaders refer to lay leaders, that does not necessarily make the case to be political. After all, even the cultic leaders were involved in this unfaithfulness (Ezra 10:18). Also, even if the term "assembly of exiles" is understood as a political community, it would not completely exclude the sense of the Ezra community being cultic as well. Instead, the narrative indicates that the community is seen primarily as a cultic community.

---

31. In some other biblical references that disapprove marriages with non-Israelites, the reason is given—such as the foreign wives/spouses leading them to apostasy (Deut 7:4; Exod 34:16; 1 Kgs 11:4–5).

32. Oswald, "Foreign Marriages and Citizenship," 2–5.

Others look at the issue from a sociological lens. For instance, Daniel Smith-Christopher argues that the only basis for Ezra's objection to the mixed marriage is that the so-called foreigners were simply Jews who were not in exile.[33] However, strictly speaking, there is not enough evidence to prove that the so-called foreigners are simply non-exiled Jews.

Some have tried to draw parallels from modern day theories. For example, Tamara Eskenazi and Eleanore Judd compare the issue with Israeli *haredi* laws and argue that the foreign wives in Ezra 9–10 could have been those who had not been exiled and thereby appropriate marriage partners but became unwanted when Ezra introduced stringent laws.[34] This argument looks appealing, but the text itself is just not clear about the identity of the foreign women.

Still others see the passage as an indication of acceptance, not denial, of the foreign wives. For instance, Yonina Dor[35] and also Sara Japhet[36] are convinced that the sending away of foreign wives in Ezra 9–10 is "on paper" and never carried out. As such, the argument goes, the events of sending away foreign wives become symbolic ceremonies for accepting them or elevating their status, who were simply "secondary wives" earlier because of their foreign status.

Finally, a more recent interpretation of Ezra 9–10 is that of Katherine Southwood. Southwood, taking an anthropological approach, identifies Ezra 9–10 as mirroring a return migration group trying to protect their ethnic identity.[37] Again, as she herself asserts, terms such as ethnicity can

---

33. Smith-Christopher claims evidence for his argument from two points: (i) the presence of texts more lenient towards foreigners (Isa 60:1–5; Ruth; Jonah), and (ii) the fact that the groups with which these "mixed" marriages are taking place are identified with old terms that have become stereotypically pejorative slurs for those ethnic groups who long have disappeared. See Smith-Christopher, "Mixed Marriage Crisis," 257.

34. Eskenazi and Judd, "Marriage to a Stranger," 266–85.

35. Dor, "Rite of Separation."

36. Japhet, "Expulsion of the Foreign Women."

37. Katherine Southwood provides a very helpful comprehensive survey of the research literature on Ezra 9–10. Some other proposed explanations for the strong disapproval of intermarriage in Ezra 9–10 includes fear of religious syncretism, inheritance and land property, female inheritance threat, land rights in connection with Persian administration, class and economic class competition. In response to these arguments, as Southwood rightly responds, there is no mention of apostasy or possibility of religious conversion in the text. The text is also silent on land ownership or inheritance, and it is not possible to know the real status of the people in the international context of Persian imperial power. For a detailed survey and discussion of the arguments and rationales, see Southwood, *Ethnicity and the Mixed Marriage*, 75–122.

be a fluid and confusing term, and it is hard to apply it strictly to the *golah* community in the book of Ezra. Restrictions of space do not allow to engage with all the varied arguments that have been made to interpret Ezra 9–10. The above few examples show how this passage has provoked different interpretations from all kinds of fields. Because of the lack of external evidence for the period, staying in the text is best in understanding the message of the passage. The purpose here, then, is to explore how the characters are characterized and what the text conveys about the situation.

Characterization of the *Golah* and the "Other"

The narrative is primarily about the protagonist *golah* group, and is less interested in the "other" people who are mentioned mostly negatively and/or only inasmuch as it aids in referencing the *golah* group. Thus, the representation of the "other" people ultimately mirrors the identity of the *golah* group. For example, if the "other" people are unclean, the *golah* group is clean. As Southwood also states, the perception of the foreigners in terms of abominations ultimately reaffirms their own group as positive and valid.[38] It is then first necessary to understand how the group understands itself, presents itself in the text, in order to understand how it views "other" people.

Self-perception of the *Golah* Community

The narrative presents two ways in which the *golah* community understood itself—as a "holy seed" (Ezra 9:2) and as a "remnant" (Ezra 9:8, 13, 15). So, it is important to analyze further the terms "holy seed" and "remnant."

Holy Seed (*zeraʿ haqqodeš*):

Those who reported to Ezra about the unfaithfulness of the *golah* community stated that the holy seed has been mixed with the peoples of the land (Ezra 9:2). Thus, one way they understood themselves is as the *holy seed* (Ezra 9:2). "Holy" in the current context would best be understood in the sense of being set apart for YHWH or belonging to YHWH.[39] Understand-

---

38. Southwood, *Ethnicity and the Mixed Marriage*, 139–40.
39. One of the meanings of "holy" is to be consecrated, to be set apart (BDB 871–72;

ing the term as "being set apart" fits their expectation to "keep themselves apart" from the peoples of the lands (Ezra 9:1). The *golah* community is often evaluated by whether or not they have "kept themselves apart from the people/s of the land/s" (Ezra 6:21; 9:1). The overriding theme of the book of Ezra is that the *golah* group is a "set apart" group, meant not to mingle with "other" people (for instance, Ezra 3:3; 4:3; 6:21). Thus, from a literary point of view, the term "holy" in the book of Ezra has the sense of being set apart from "others," set apart for YHWH.

Outside of Ezra 9–10 the term "holy" (*qodeš*) is also used to mean "being set apart." For example, when the priests are said to be "holy" it designates their relation to YHWH (Aaron and his sons [Exod 28:36; 39:30; Lev 21:6]). The Israelites themselves are set apart for YHWH. In Exod 22:30, the Israelites are to maintain a ritual diet as they are set apart for YHWH. In Jer 2:3, the Israelites are "holy" to YHWH, thus set apart as the first fruits of YHWH's harvest. In Isa 62:12 Israel is "holy" for YHWH, that is, set apart as redeemed by YHWH. Such a status also comes with the obligation to maintain that status. In other words, holiness is not an innate or immutable condition, but human response and maintenance of that status is necessary. As holy people set apart for YHWH, they are to emulate YHWH and keep apart from those who are not YHWH's people.[40]

The term "seed" (*zeraʿ*) is oriented towards the future. It refers to offspring, children or descendants: for instance, the seed of woman (Eve) that refers to humankind (Gen 3:15); the seed of Abraham (Gen 13:15–16; 16:10; 22:17); the seed of the patriarchs to refer to their descendants (Exod 32:13; 33:1; Josh 24:3); children (Lev 18:21; 20:2); seed of Abraham that refers to Israelites (Isa 41:8; Ps 105:6; Jer 33:26; 2 Chr 20:7). In the context of Ezra 9:2, it is used as a self-designation for the *golah* community, implying that they understood themselves as the seed, that is, descendants, of pre-exilic Israel (Ezra 9:6–8:13). With no mention of people who remained in the land—who might be lumped together into the group "peoples of the lands"—it appears that the *golah* group sees themselves as constituents of the pre-exilic Israelite community.

Clines, *Dictionary of Classical Hebrew*, 198–99). In a more specific sense, David Clines convincingly argues that the term means belonging to God. He comes to this meaning from examining the occurrences of the root *qdš* in the Hebrew Bible and their usage/meaning in those contexts. See Clines, *Alleged Basic Meanings*.

40. Harrington, "Interpreting Leviticus," 215.

The only other place in the Hebrew Bible where the phrase "holy seed" is found is in Isa 6:13, where the phrase represents a rebirth of life.[41] Even after the tree fell, the stump remains which will sprout again; that is, even after near total destruction or exile, the stump of Israel remains—the holy seed, that will revive, representing the emergence of a faithful remnant, which springs after Israel's destruction, a new creation of God.[42] Thus, while there is widespread destruction of cities, of houses and fields, of social and political institutions, and Israel had left its own land, there is still hope for survival and the revival of a remnant, a holy seed that will spring up from the stump.[43] There is also hope for renewal beyond judgment.[44] Such is the self-understanding of the *golah* community in Ezra 9–10 as well (Ezra 9:8; 10:2b).

Becking also rightly points out how the term "holy seed" is largely a radical self-interpretation of the *golah* group as being elected by God, implying that they cannot be defiled by foreign elements.[45] He asserts that the term really is a combination of two traditional depictions of Israel—that is, Israel is called a "holy nation" in Deuteronomy, and the "seed of Abraham" elsewhere. As discussed above in the individual terms "holy" and "seed," the *golah* group highlighted their continuity of pre-exilic Israel ("seed of Abraham") and how they have to set themselves apart for YHWH ("holy nation"). The *golah* community subscribed to both traditions in their self-perception.

In sum, the *golah* community understood itself as a "holy seed"—a community set apart for YHWH, set apart from others. This understanding explains the core criterion for membership in their community as to "have kept oneself separated from the (uncleanness of) the people/s of the land/s."[46] This self-understanding of the *golah* community as "set apart for YHWH" also correlates with their self-understanding of being a "remnant saved by YHWH."

---

41. While there are textual difficulties, we can make sense out of it. The text is thus commonly understood to present an element of hope and renewal. See, for instance, Childs, *Isaiah*, 58; Roberts, *First Isaiah*, 101.

42. Childs, *Isaiah*, 54–59.

43. Watts, *Isaiah 1–33*, 109–10.

44. Roberts, *First Isaiah*, 101.

45. Becking, "On the Identity," 32.

46. "All those who have separated themselves . . . to join" (Ezra 6:21) the *golah* community were welcome in the Passover celebration. In Ezra 9:1, some people failed to maintain that criterion of separating themselves and ended up committing an unfaithfulness.

Rebuilding of the *Golah* Community under Ezra

Remnant (*pĕlêṭâ*):

The *golah* community also understood their status as being the remnant (Ezra 9:8, 13–15). Ezra repeatedly states in his prayer how the *golah* community would still commit an unfaithfulness by marrying peoples who followed abominable practices, even after they were being granted status as a remnant (Ezra 9:13–14).

The term remnant has mainly a salvific underpinning referring back to the rescuing of Israelites and Judeans in the larger catastrophe of Judah and Israel. Being left, spared or saved (as a remnant) is a concept for future survival. A short survey of the occurrences of the concept outside of Ezra 9–10 will be helpful to derive a general meaning of the term. In 2 Kgs 17:18, after the fall of Samaria (722 BCE), everything was destroyed except for the tribe of Judah.[47] In Jer 50:20, YHWH declares that those spared will be pardoned. In Zeph 3:12, the poor and humble folk who will find refuge in the name of YHWH. In Judg 21:17, a remnant will be there so that the tribe of Benjamin may not be blotted out. Joel 3:5 mentions that those who invoke the name of YHWH shall escape and be a remnant on Mount Zion and Jerusalem. In Jer 44:14, many will not survive the sword, famine and pestilence but a few remnant will return to Judah. Isaiah 10:20–23 speaks of a small remnant of Israel from destruction that will be leaning on YHWH. In Isa 37:31–32, the remnant of Judah will rise and develop again by renewing its root below and producing fruit above. In Isa 4:2–3, a remnant that are left in Zion and in Jerusalem will be called "holy," and in Isa 6:13, the remnant that will sprout again after the towns, houses and the population are destroyed will be a holy seed. It can be seen from the above references that those left as "remnant" are not left or spared randomly, but are saved purposefully by YHWH. The concept of an Israelite remnant is not limited to escapees from religious or political struggles, but also secures the future existence of the people after a breakdown; a remnant of people faithful to YHWH, representing the true Israel.[48] Thus, the term "remnant," though it may be used in different contexts to refer to different people, connotates of being spared by the mercy of YHWH purposefully.

---

47. Other references include 2 Kgs 25:22, which talks about those left after many were exiled to Babylon, and 1 Kgs 19:18, which states that YHWH will spare seven thousand who did not kneel before Baal. See also Gen 45:7; 2 Sam 15:14; 2 Kgs 19:20; 2 Chr 12:7; 30:6.

48. Hasel, "*pĕlêṭâ*" (*TDOT* 11:563).

It may not be possible to specify from which reference/s Ezra 9–10 borrows its usage of the term remnant. It is clear, however, that Ezra 9–10 refers to the *golah* community as the remnant, and the connotations of the term as observed in other references are also true of Ezra 9–10. Surviving destruction, as in the case of the *golah* community, also would lead them to firmer loyalty to YHWH and the Torah in order to sustain their remnant status. Ezra accounted how YHWH God has granted them as a remnant and has given them a stake in his holy place, even after all their sufferings because of their iniquities (Ezra 9:8, 13–15). The term remnant is used to refer to the *golah* community, that is, primarily those who were exiled and then returned.[49] The term also systematically excludes any reference to those who remained in the land. As a remnant, the *golah* community understood itself as a small portion being spared and saved out of widespread destruction to begin a new life dependent on YHWH.

The text also states that besides being a remnant the *golah* community is also given a "stake" (*yātēd*) (Ezra 9:8). Literally, a "stake in his holy place" would be their status in the Temple. The metaphor of being given a stake in his holy place (Ezra 9:8) would mean being given some kind of stability or security, through the temple rebuilt, at least for a brief moment.[50] But, being given a stake also expresses vulnerability and thus dependence on YHWH, as Moffat argues.[51] In the context of Ezra 9–10, the *golah* community is in a vulnerable situation because of their unfaithfulness, and Ezra's prayer clearly points to the imminent danger of YHWH's wrath the community faces because of the intermarriage issue (Ezra 9:6–15). First, that "stake" has been given for just a moment. Secondly, that security was solely

---

49. Generally, post-exilic literatures tend to view the remnant as centered in Babylon, that is, those exiled to Babylon who then later returned to Judah, and Jerusalem is viewed as the periphery. On the other hand, pre-exilic literatures center the remnant on Jerusalem and view Babylon as the periphery. See Rom-Shiloni, *Exclusive Inclusivity*, 87–89.

50. The metaphor of the "stake (or tent peg) in holy place" can be understood in two ways. First, in a nomadic way of life, a secure tent peg meant stability for the tent and thereby the occupants (Isa 54:2). Secondly, it can also be understood in how a person is compared to a peg fixed in a firm place and said to be able hold the whole family together (Isa 22:23). See Williamson, *Ezra, Nehemiah*, 135.

51. Moffat argues how the "stake" speaks more of insecurity or vulnerability rather than firm security. He argues that while the stake/peg metaphor in Isa 22 can indeed mean firmness or security, the context is more of the vulnerability of the peg, as the peg on which the family of Eliakim holds on to will fall once the Divine cut it off (Isa 22:23–25). See Moffat, "Metaphor at Stake," 290–98. In a similar manner, the "stake" of the *golah* community is fully dependent on YHWH, which could fall if they keep committing unfaithfulness against YHWH.

dependent on YHWH, as it was only by the mercy and favor of YHWH that such a stake has been given. Because they have failed, and despite being spared as a remnant and given a stake, they could easily lose that favor too (see Ezra 9:14). Even though being given a stake implies security, the people were vulnerable in the sense that their actions could result in losing that security/stake again. Thus, being spared as a remnant and given a stake come with responsibilities. When the future is not secure, the remnant that is spared depends on God and they must carefully follow God to sustain and revive the community.

The "brightening of our eyes" also literally would mean a sign of gaining physical strength and freshness, so as to renew life. Metaphorically, it would refer to the new hope the community receives, a sign of their revived life after being in prolonged bondage. Ezra stated (rhetorically) how God would finally have a rage against them and destroy them if even after being spared as a remnant they still violated YHWH's command by intermarrying with the people who followed abominable practices (Ezra 9:14). The remnant *golah* community thus depended on the mercy of YHWH for their survival and continuity and could not afford to do what would not be acceptable to YHWH.

The two self-conceptions of the *golah* community that are presented in the text—a holy seed (Ezra 9:2) and a remnant (Ezra 9:8, 13–15)—are interconnected. Both concepts understand the community as one that is set apart for YHWH to continue the community as the true Israel through absolute loyalty and obedience to YHWH. This self-perception of the *golah* community also frames their view towards "other" people. That is, the stringent view on intermarriage would have come first and preeminently from their desire to maintain their self-perception as a set apart community of YHWH, spared as a remnant to continue Israel into the future. Their self-conception as a holy seed and a remnant would have cautioned them to mix with any "other" people whose lifestyles are abominable, like non-Yahwistic nations.

The Unfaithfulness of the *Golah* Community

The self-perception of the *golah* community as the holy seed and the remnant obliged them to keep themselves apart, thereby failing that expectation became an unfaithfulness, *ma'al*. That is, the *golah* community have committed an unfaithfulness by not keeping themselves apart from the peoples of the lands whose abominations were like the stereotyped non-Yahwistic nations and even marrying their women (Ezra 9:1–2). This unfaithfulness is also disobedience of YHWH's commandments (*miṣwôt* [Ezra 9:10, 14; 10:3]). The term for unfaithfulness, *ma'al*, is used in this context as the failure to remain apart, which eventually led them even to marry those from whom they should keep themselves apart.

In other appearances of the term *ma'al*, it is often against God. While in some instances the term may express trespass against the holy temple (2 Chr 26:16–18; 28:19–25) or violation of oath taken in YHWH's name (Lev 20:3; 26:15; Isa 57:15) or against other humans (Num 5:6), the common denominator of *ma'al* is against God.[52] That is, a *ma'al* is an act of disobedience to YHWH, whether the action itself may take different forms. In Ezra 9–10, as the *golah* community perceived themselves as the ones belonging to YHWH to continue Israel into the future, their failure to keep themselves apart from "other" people who did not follow YHWH's ways is unfaithfulness. Such an unfaithfulness could endanger their identity and ability to remain being of YHWH and to continue the life of Israel into the future.

Unfaithfulness also could lead to YHWH's wrath against the whole community even when it is committed by some individuals as seen in Ezra 9–10 where some *golah* men's unfaithfulness is seen to affect the whole community.[53] As such, all the *golah* community should keep themselves apart from the peoples of the lands who have abominations unacceptable to YHWH and thus for the *golah* community.

Problem with the Peoples of the Lands

What is it about "other" people—the people/s of the lands or foreign women—that is so unacceptable that the *golah* community should remain apart from them? The text states that the abominations of the peoples of the lands are *like* those of the nations of the Canaanites, the Hittites, the Perizzites, the Jebusites, the Ammonites, the Moabites, the Egyptians and the Amorites (Ezra 9:1). The text also states that they have uncleanness (Ezra

---

52. Milgrom, "Concept of Ma'al," 236–39.

53. In other appearances also similar cases are observable. Achan's unfaithfulness brought God's wrath on the whole community (Josh 22:20), King Ahaz's unfaithfulness led to subjugation of Judah (2 Chr 28:19), and Israel will be taken in exile because of the king's unfaithfulness (Ezek 17:19–21).

9:11). The *golah* community have failed to keep themselves apart from the peoples of the lands whose abominations were like some non-Yahwistic nations. From the use of the preposition *kĕ* it is clear that the peoples of the lands are not equated with the nations listed, but are rather only likened to.[54] These peoples are said to have abominations like those of the stereotyped non-Yahwistic nations.

A study of "abomination" (*tôʿēbâ*) particularly when used in reference to other nations, reveals it to be actions or lifestyles that are immoral and unacceptable to YHWH. Such abominable actions include both the cultic and ethical realms. For instance, the term refers to sexual immorality, child sacrifice, profaning God's name (Lev 18:26–30); divination, witchcraft, necromancy and such, which are regarded as practices of Canaanite nations (Deut 18:9–12; 20:17–18); idol worship (Deut 7:25–26; 12:29–31; 2 Kgs 21:1–9); worship of Baal (Jer 2:7).[55] Such actions or lifestyles are those that YHWH worshippers are prohibited from doing. They are actions that are irreconcilable with YHWH, contrary to the will and character of YHWH; abominable acts are like taboos ethically and cultically.[56] Thus, while it may not be possible to strictly narrow down "abominations" into a single list of specific actions in Ezra 9–10, the term would generally mean cultic action such as idolatry and other unethical actions such as sexual immorality. The peoples of the lands are then said to live such lifestyles. In fact, the text refers to these peoples directly with their abominations—"the people of these abominations" (Ezra 9:14). The *golah* community should remain apart from those who have such abominable lifestyles.

Another noted problem with the peoples of the lands is their uncleanness. The term for "uncleanness," *niddâ*, would be figurative in this context, as it relates to human unethical lifestyles: "A land unclean with the uncleanness of the peoples of the lands" (Ezra 9:11).[57] In Ezra 9:11, the land is

---

54. As Brown also points out, the preposition *kĕ* in Ezra 9:1 establishes a comparison rather than identifying them with those nations. See Brown, "Problem of Mixed Marriages," 447.

55. When in reference to Israelites also, the term has similar connotation of cultic actions and ethical lifestyles, including offerings to other gods or idol worship (Jer 16:18–20; 44:4, 22–23; Deut 27:15; 32:16; 2 Kgs 16:3), profaning the sanctuary and marrying daughter of foreign god (Mal 2:11); sexual immorality, injustice, robbery, murder, idolatry (Ezek 5:9; 7:3–4, 8–9; 16:36, 50, 58; 18:12–13; 22:11; 33:26); whoredom, sexual immorality, and dishonesty (Deut 23:18–19; 24:4; 25:13–16); child offering and idolatry (2 Kgs 16:3; 21:2–4, 11).

56. Preuss, "*tôʿēbâ*" (*TDOT* 15:602).

57. The term could mean ceremonial uncleanness (such as menstruation of women

compared to a woman who becomes unclean, a *niddâ*, during and because of her menstruation.⁵⁸ That is, it indicates that the land has become unclean because of the abominable lifestyles of those who inhabited it, lifestyles unacceptable to the *golah* people, holy and set apart for YHWH. Thus, the term is used in a metaphorical sense and denotes differences between the *golah* and "others."⁵⁹ Not only the people but even the land has become detestable because of the detestable lifestyles of those who inhabited it. The *golah* people should therefore keep away from such people. Similarly, the term for "impurity," *ṭumʾâ*, would also refer to impurity through ethical (such as sexual) and religious practices (such as idolatry) (Num 5:19; Lev 16:16; 18; Ezek 22:13–15; 24:13–14; 36:25, 29).⁶⁰

Thus, from the text it is their abominations primarily that is problematic about the peoples of the land/s and the foreign women. More precisely, it is their abominable lifestyles and resulting unclean position from unacceptable lifesyles. For this very reason, the *golah* community, being the community set apart to continue the life of Israel into the future, should not follow such lifestyles and could not accept anyone who followed such lifestyles, which also compelled them to do away with what they perceived was incompatible for their community.

Send Away Foreign Wives and their Children (Ezra 10:3–44)

The *golah* community had committed an unfaithfulness by failing to keep themselves apart from the peoples of the lands and intermarrying with

---

[Ezek 18:6; 22:10; 36:17; Lev 12:2; 15:19–25], taking brother's wife [Lev 20:21], or of a corpse [Num 19:9–21]). The term could also be figurative—particularly in reference to idolatry (2 Chr 29:5; Zech 13:1; Ezek 7:19–20).

58. Erbele-Küster, studying the term particularly in Lev 15, argues that in Lev 15:19, *niddâ* would be a technical term for cultic position caused by blood flow. Thus the words "her discharge being blood" indicates a physical phenomenon, while the term *niddâ* is more of a cultic description. Furthermore, the duration of blood flow is variable, while *niddâ* by definition lasts for seven days, that is, the period of exclusion from the sacred because of the discharge will last seven days regardless of the actual length of menstruation. As such, *niddâ* expresses cultic uncleanness. See Erbele-Küster, *Body, Gender, and Purity*, 120–21.

59. Erbele-Küster, *Body, Gender, and Purity*, 123.

60. These terms "uncleanness" and "impurity" are rarely used of non-Israelites. Thus, searching for the implication of "uncleanness of the peoples of the land" from other biblical references does not help much.

them (Ezra 9:1–2). In order to resolve this unfaithfulness, the proposed solution was to send away the foreign women and their children (Ezra 10:3), and the community responded accordingly (Ezra 10:5–44). As the people gathered before Ezra to solve their unfaithfulness, they were told to make confession to YHWH, to do YHWH's will and to keep themselves apart from the peoples of the land and the foreign women (Ezra 10:11). The people responded by pledging to follow the command (Ezra 10:12). Ezra and the leaders then collected the names of the men, both cultic people—priestly families, Levites, temple personnel, and lay people who had brought home foreign women (Ezra 10:16–44). Anyone who did not show up within three days would be separated from the community and their properties would be confiscated (Ezra 10:8). This means that not just the foreign women but any men who failed to abide by the remedial measures of their unfaithfulness risked being excommunicated from their community. This excommunication would give them equal status with non-*golah* people, such as the foreign women and the peoples of the lands who were unacceptable to them (Ezra 9:1; 10:11). In other words, anyone not willing to show up to fix the unfaithfulness of their community can no longer be a part of this group. There is no evidence provided in the text for strong and major oppositions for the proposed solution. As the proposed solution in Ezra 9–10 is quite strong and even unprecedented, with no prescribed law or example to follow, it is thus open to various explanations.

Wrestling with the Solution

The proposal of Shecaniah, inspired by Ezra ("my lord") and those who tremble at the commandment of God, is also said to be "according to the law." But there is no known Pentateuchal law that commands the divorce of foreign wife.[61] As is usual in the larger narrative, it does not seem to be referring to a specific set of written laws, but could rather be an interpretation of a general law or teachings or tradition,[62] and attempts to locate a specific law is unnecessary. Rather, what it reveals about the *golah* community is their earnestness to follow the law and commands of YHWH (at least in the way they understood) and to correct their mistake.

---

61. While it is forbidden to marry some Canaanite nationals (Deut 7:3–4), no mandates about divorce of foreign women in general is attested.

62. Fried, *Ezra*, 395.

Rebuilding a Post-exilic Community

The strong resolution proposed to send away their foreign wives and children has attracted several explanations. A recent attempt to make sense of the solution is that of Csilla Saysell. Saysell argues that the solution is in fact not so harsh as it might seem, considering what might be required by the law. She compares Ezra 9–10 with the *ḥērem* law, which affected mostly two groups of people—Idolatrous Israelites (Exod 22:19; Lev 27:29; Deut 13:13–18) and the seven Canaanite nations (Deut 20:16–18; Josh 10:28, 37, 39).[63] Saysell argues that the proposed solution in Ezra 10 could be a re-interpretation of the *ḥērem* law in the metaphorical sense by the postexilic community, and in that sense, it actually is a less harsh option. Yet, as Saysell herself notes, the situation in Ezra 9–10 is different in some ways. For instance, while in the *ḥērem* law, the person bringing an idol into the community would also be banned, in Ezra 9–10, the men who brought the foreign women were not put away. Furthermore, and more importantly, a different term *bādal* (Niphal) is used in Ezra, instead of the term *ḥērem*.

While Saysell reads it as a less harsh option from actual Pentateuchal ban laws, others such as Yonina Dor and Sara Japhet view the event as a positive one. Dor argues that the event of sending away foreign women meant an acceptance of the "other" people. Dor comes to this view from a literary-textual analysis that the text records only a publication of the list (Ezra 10) without any mention or no indication of actually sending away the wives and children. Thus, for Dor, the separation events were "merely symbolic ceremonies or rituals that were meant to enable accepting of outsiders into the community."[64]

Japhet argues along similar lines for the legal basis of the solution. Japhet argues that when women are of inferior status, they take the fate of their mother, not father.[65] For instance, Japhet argues, Sarah was legally able to demand that Abraham send Hagar away because of two features of Hagar—her Egyptian origin and her status as a slave-woman (Gen 21:9–23). Ishmael is also identified from his mother Hagar as "the son of the slave-woman" (Gen 21:10, 13). Also, the sons of Abraham with his wife Keturah are identified as "sons of the concubine" (Gen 25:6). Furthermore, the laws of Hebrew slaves dictate that if the master gives the slave a wife,

---

63. Saysell, *According to the Law*, 58–80.

64. Dor further speculates that the first returnees probably took those wives considering them to be Israelites and only later found out that these wedlocks are condemned as sinful after the establishment of separatist group. See Dor, "Rite of Separation," 174–86.

65. Japhet, "Expulsion of the Foreign Women," 100.

the children of the slave take their status from their mother (not father), and even when the slave goes free, the wife and children would still belong to the master (Exod 21:3–4). Japhet finds a common denominator in these three cases—a slave, a concubine and a possession of the master—that all these women are of inferior status, and that their children take the fate of their mothers. Japhet then argues that these three similar cases provide the analogous legal framework for the proposed solution in Ezra 9–10 (Ezra 10:2). She justifies that a conventional divorce procedure is not necessary because the foreign women are of inferior status, and counted as "secondary wives," and "the problem faced by the people of Judah was not the women's faith or religious behavior, but their origin."[66] Thus, for Japhet, this solution is an innovation for an unprecedented situation, where the foreign women are elevated with slave women, and the sending away of foreign wives event in Ezra 9–10 becomes one of the factors that facilitated the idea and practice of conversion.[67]

While arguments such as those stated above are appealing, there is just not enough evidence, particularly in the text. More importantly, the text does not pin point only women or foreign women, but commands the whole *golah* community to keep themselves apart from the peoples of the land/s (Ezra 9:1; 10:2–3, 11). Thus, the solution has to do not just with foreign wives but it should have something to do with all "other" people.

The Solution in Perspective of the Whole Narrative

The situation in Ezra 9–10 and the way the *golah* community handled the situation they found themselves in are unprecented and sound quite radical, but they can be made sense of when considered within the perspective of the whole narrative. The *golah* community's understanding of their situation and their self-perception of their own community are the determining factors in how they handled the situation.

I have argued that the *golah* community understood their unfaithfulness as their failure to keep themselves apart and mingling with the peoples of the land/s and even marrying foreign women from the peoples of the land/s. This unfaithfulness was understood as a disobedience of God's command (Ezra 9:10, 14; 10:2–3), and the proposed solution of sending away the foreign wives and their children was also understood as an obedience to

---

66. Japhet, "Expulsion of the Foreign Women," 151–52, 154.
67. Japhet, "Expulsion of the Foreign Women," 156, 161.

the Torah (Ezra 10:3). Also, though the unfaithfulness was not committed by all members or all men, the whole community was understood to be affected such that the whole community has to respond to YHWH (Ezra 9:4; 10:1, 9, 12), in pledging to send away the foreign wives and to obey the Torah (Ezra 10:3), as well as in remaining apart from the peoples of the land and foreign women (Ezra 10:11). The difficulty, however, is that while there are stipulations in the Torah discouraging marriage to non-Israelites, there are no explicit measures laid out to respond if one breaks them. For instance, in Deut 7:1–4, Israelites are told not to intermarry with the Canaanite nations because they will turn them to apostasy, but there is no mention of how to respond if someone fails to obey the command. In the event of Ezra 9–10, the proposed solution to the unfaithfulness of marrying foreign women was to put out their spouses (Ezra 10:3, 19). And this was what they understood to be in accordance to the Torah (Ezra 10:3).

More importantly, the *golah* community's self-perception of who they were and their status or responsibility seem to have driven the solution they came up with. As a group that understood itself to be a group "set apart for YHWH" ("holy seed" [Ezra 9:2]) and a remnant (Ezra 9:8, 13–15), everyone has to abide closely by the community standards and expectations. As such, separation would have seemed the only option and that sprung from their rigid self-perception. In fact, keeping oneself separated from "other" who were not part of the *golah* community and who followed abominable lifestyles unacceptable to YHWH has been the expected criterion for the *golah* community throughout the whole narrative.

Conclusion

From what the text presents, the community perceived itself as a holy seed—set apart for and belonging to YHWH, and as a remnant—purposefully saved from destruction to continue Israel into the future. From these two self-understandings derive the main criteria to be part of the community—to maintain being a holy seed and to fulfill being a remnant, and thereby to keep oneself apart from "others" who have lifestyles unacceptable to YHWH and the *golah* community. The "other" people—people/s of the lands and "foreign women"—have abominations, which though not specified by the text include cultic and ethical realms such as idolatry and sexual immorality. Such abominations were unacceptable for the Yahwistic *golah* community. As such, people (women) with such abominations would have to be removed from among their community. The narrative is primarily about the protagonist *golah* community whose self-understanding as a holy seed and a remnant—set apart for YHWH—were now being threatened. They have failed to maintain their criteria by failing to remain apart and intermarrying "other" women and they must have felt that the only solution was to remove what was unacceptable to them, what they have been commanded to keep away from.

The situation of the *golah* community could also have partly contributed to their strongly negative attitude and action toward these "other" people. While they had insecurities in the earlier parts of the narrative causing them to have dread of "other" people (Ezra 3) and not allowing them to join in their temple builing (Ezra 4), after the temple was built they must have become so secure as a community and ended up compromising of their own standards.

5

Conclusion

THIS STUDY IS A literary analysis of the book of Ezra in its final form, reading it synchronically with the main focus on the identifications and encounter of the protagonist *golah* group with the antagonist "other" group. After an overall survey of the whole book (chapter 1), the accounts of the particular interactions between the two groups are studied (chapters 2–4). At the end, two findings emerge. The first is on what the narrative is about. The second discusses whether there is a coherent basis for the seemingly inconsistent attitudes towards the "other," some hostile (Ezra 4:1–5; 9–10), some welcoming (Ezra 6:19–22).

What is the Narrative About?

Clearly, the narrative is primarily about the *golah* community. The book of Ezra reveals complexities including the implementation of different genres of narrative, Hebrew-Aramaic bilingualism, the appearance of the figure Ezra only in later half of the book. The text also apparently draws ideologies from different traditions, such as the Torah, Deuteronomic, priestly or even prophetic, without strictly or exclusively following one particular tradition. Nevertheless, despite these apparent complexities, one common theme runs throughout the narrative. The narrative is primarily about the *golah* community, while all non-*golah* people are tentatively seen collectively as the "other."

The *golah* community receives proper identifications, with the main terms used for their identification being the *golah* (Ezra 2:1; 4:1; 6:16,

19–21; 8:35; 10:6–7, 16) and Israel (Ezra 2:2; 3:1; 6:16–17, 21; 7:7, 13; 8:25; 9:1, 4; 10:5, 10). As such, the protagonist group is mainly constituted by those who returned from the exile and they perceived themselves as the "holy seed" set apart for YHWH, set apart from "other" people and as the remnant to continue preexilic Israel into the future. On the other hand, the antagonist "other" people receive unspecific identifications and are mentioned only with respect to the *golah* group, positively or negatively. Except for some named persons such as the Persian kings Cyrus (Ezra 1:1–2), Ahasuerus (Ezra 4:6), Artaxerxes (Ezra 4:7), Darius (Ezra 6), Persian officials (Ezra 4:7–9; 5:3; 6:6), or the Sidonians and Tyrians (Ezra 3:7), other designations are vague. "Other" people are identified by terms such as "peoples of the lands" (Ezra 3:3; 9:1–2, 11), "people of the land" (Ezra 4:4), "peoples of the land" (Ezra 10:2, 11), "nations of the land" (Ezra 6:21), "adversaries of Judah and Benjamin" (Ezra 4:1), foreign (Ezra 10:2, 10). The terms used for "other" people rather serve as their characterization and are often left with no further information. As such, all non-*golah* people form one broad group of "other" which will encompass anyone, inclusive of both non-exiled Jews and non-Jews. In simple terms, for the narrative, there are only two kinds of people—the *golah* community and "other" non-*golah* people. Some "other" people who supported them, such as the Persian kings Cyrus and Darius, though not portrayed negatively, were also not a part of their community. Thus, the narrative is about the *golah* community.

Varying Attitudes towards the "Other"

In the book of Ezra, different attitudes towards the "other" can be observed. Some are quite negative such as dread (Ezra 3:3), adversity (Ezra 4:1), or even chasing them away (Ezra 9–10). On the other hand, there is an account where "other" people are welcome (Ezra 6:21). As such, there seems inconsistency in their attitude towards the "other."

In the first account, as the *golah* community arrived in the land the "other" people, designated as peoples of the lands, caused them dread while they were building the altar (Ezra 3:3). Then, as they started rebuilding the temple, their "adversaries" proposed to join them in building the temple (Ezra 4:1–2). The *golah* leaders, however, rejected their proposal to build together (Ezra 4:3), and later the "other" people thwarted the building work of the temple, causing a halt in their work (Ezra 4:4–5).

The building work was resumed with the inspiration of the prophets (Ezra 5:1–2) and the temple was completed and dedicated (6:15–17), despite obstacles (Ezra 5:3–17). Then, the Passover was celebrated, and for the first time in the narrative "other" people were welcome to join them. All those who had kept themselves apart from the uncleanness of the nations were allowed to join them in the Passover to worship YHWH (Ezra 6:21).

At the end of the narrative we find the most hostile attitude towards the "other." After Ezra and some more people returned from the exile, the community was convicted of failing to separate themselves from "other" people and even marrying foreign women. The community then was firmly ordered to keep themselves apart from "other" people and to send away all their foreign wives and their children (Ezra 9–10).

Thus, there are different attitudes towards the "other," mostly negative. The analysis of the whole narrative, however, reveals that there is a consistent basis that decides the attitude towards the "other."

A Coherent Theme behind the Varying Attitudes

Through the seemingly inconsistent attitude or varying degrees of hostility towards the "other," there indeed is a coherent basis, though not always explicitly stated. The *golah* community viewed themselves apart from "other" people, who was seen to have abominations and thus unacceptable to be a part of the *golah* community. The varying degrees of hostility towards the "other" in the book of Ezra can be explained while maintaining this consistent expectation. The "other" people could be non-exiled Jews or non-Jews.

The first account of the *golah* community's encounter of "other" people where they were in dread of the "other" people (Ezra 3:3) can be understood as follows. The first group of people who returned to Jerusalem started to settle in the towns (Ezra 2:70; 3:1) and built the altar, followed by cultic activities such as making sacrifices and celebrating festivals (Ezra 3:2–6). During this phase of settling and first cultic activities, they felt the dread of the "other" (Ezra 3:3). It would only be natural for the *golah* group, who recently returned to the land, to have insecurities and difficulties as they were settling themselves back on to this land "new" to them after a long period in exile. They would also have difficulty fitting back into the culture, social or cultic, and would have found differences between them and those who remained in the land. As such, dread of "other" people would have easily emerged on the *golah* community. The *golah* community also had mixed

Conclusion

emotions as they celebrated the temple foundation (Ezra 3:10–13). In all these events, and clearly at the celebration of the temple foundation "other" people were simply onlookers or hearers from afar (Ezra 3:13).

In the second account of the *golah* community encountering "other" people, the relationship is presented even more negatively—as adversarial (Ezra 4:1–2). Have those whom they were in dread of earlier (Ezra 3:3) now turned to be their adversaries? Although it cannot be known whether it involved the exact same people (Ezra 3:3; 4:1), the narrative presents that the *golah* people now have "adversaries." Even though these "adversaries" claimed to worship the *golah's* God ("*your* God" [Ezra 4:2]), the *golah* leaders denied their proposal by saying that they alone will build the house ("of *our* God") as authorized by Cyrus (Ezra 4:3). That is, the *golah* community kept themselves apart from "other" people and built alone. Even though the *golah* community would have been more settled by this time, with the temple building just commencing, they would have still had some sense of insecurity. Evidently, they desired to be cautious—to fulfill that they were the ones authorized by the Persian king. Furthermore, those "other" did not seem to be cultically identical to them.

The strongest affirmative attitude towards the "other" is seen in the Passover account after the completion and dedication of the temple where certain "other" people were welcomed (Ezra 6:21). How has the *golah* community now become open to "other" people? First, they were not random "other" people but who, like the *golah* people themselves, had kept themselves apart from the uncleanness of the nations and joined them to worship YHWH. The *golah* community maintained that same requirement of keeping themselves apart from "other" people, and these people had met that prerequisite. Second, having built the temple and the temple services re-installed (Ezra 6:18), it could be that the *golah* community were settled and more confidently established, compared to the earlier times of their arrival and temple building, and that would have made easier for them to be welcoming to "other" people.

The most hostile attitude towards the "other" is in Ezra 9–10 where the *golah* community is accused of unfaithfulness by failing to keep themselves apart from "other" people and marrying their women (Ezra 9:1–2). The community then resolved to send away their foreign wives and their children (Ezra 10). As hostile as the resolution seems, the core requirement of the *golah* community remains the same as in the earlier part of the narrative—that they should keep themselves apart from the "other." It could be that with the temple re-installed, they felt even more settled and secure. Between the community' reestablishment, in particular the gratified moment with the re-installed temple, and the time of Ezra 9–10, they had become lenient and compromising of their requirement and consequently failed. Later, after studying the law they came to realize their failure, and a strict interpretation and implementation of the law made them to delineate the criteria for the membership of and exclusion from their community. The difference between the openness in Ezra 6:21 and exclusivist attitude in Ezra 9–10 could be that the "other" people in 6:21 were those who already met the prerequisite of separating themselves from uncleanness before joining the *golah* community, whereas the "other" women in 9–10 had not met that prerequisite before being taken as wives by the *golah* men.

Thus, in all these accounts of encountering "other" people with varying attitudes towards the "other"—from dread to adversity to welcoming to chasing them away—there is one criterion behind the judgment of the attitudes. The one coherent criterion for *golah* community membership is that they should keep themselves apart from "other" people who followed abominations (Ezra 9:1, 11, 14), unless they also have kept themselves apart from such unacceptable lifestyles to seek YHWH, in which case they could become a part of the *golah* community (Ezra 6:21). The varying degrees of hostility or welcoming could also have been affected by their journey of rebuilding themselves as a community—from a newly arrived insecure and unsettled one making them negative towards "other" people to a settled and established community that even became over-confident and compromising of their standards to remain apart from "other" abominable people.

Implications for Today: A Brief Personal Reflection

While a hermeneutical reflection on alterity is beyond the scope of this study, I will briefly consider the book of Ezra's negative attitudes towards the "other" in its relevance for today. There are different options. We could not read it, since there are other books in the canon. Or, we could read only the parts that are inspiring while ignoring the difficult parts. Or, we could follow the example of the *golah* community and apply its lessons to today. I would like to propose to read the whole narrative and wrestle more particularly and diligently with the difficult parts before interpreting it and applying it to our contemporary context.

Conclusion

Coming from a minority tribe, the Paite,[1] in northeast India, there are some ways our people would resonate with the *golah* community in their particular situation. One thing I observe from the narrative is that the *golah* community's view towards the "other" largely comes from their perception of themselves. That is, their self-perceptions as the ones set apart for YHWH ("holy seed") and to continue Israel into the future after the catastrophe of the exile ("remnant"). Being a "remnant" from the exile, they were expected to keep themselves apart from "other" people. As a minority group, most Paite people feel a similar need to be distinct and preserve our distinctiveness as a Paite Christian tribe. Generally, a Paite desires to be aware of being a Paite, or at least not to forget that and live up to being a Paite (the obvious way being by upholding the traditions, language, culture, religion and such). Marrying into another tribe or ethnic group is not encouraged. And, in cases of intermarriage, it is relatively easier to be accepted if it is with another Christian (most preferably the same denomination) than a non-Christian which is highly disapproved of and in certain cases could even lead to being (virtually) disowned by family or the larger community. And, as with the *golah* community, the Paites' view of "other" people, or not encouraging intermarriage, does not necessarily stem first from a negative view of "other" people themselves, but rather from their own view of their distinctiveness as a Paite Christian tribe and to preserve that identity.

Having said that, should we take the example of the *golah* community, particularly how they dealt with their foreign wives in Ezra 9–10? The path the *golah* community took is unimaginable from a modern multicultural perspective. Certainly, it would have been hard in the biblical context too, as seen in the sending away of Hagar, where Hagar and the child suffered, and Abraham himself suffered too (Gen 21:11, 14–16). Would the path taken in Ezra 9–10 ended well for the *golah* community? How about for the women and children sent away? Would that path have redeemed the problem the *golah* community ran into?

In fact, as seen in the analysis of the text, it is not even explicitly asserted whether the wives and their children were actually sent away. The narrative ends confusingly, stating how some *golah* men married foreign

---

1. The Paite (Zomi) is one of the tribes of India, mainly living in Lamka, Churachandpur, the southern part of Manipur, even though they are spread all over the country of India and other parts of the world now. The Paite tribe as a community embraced Christianity when Welsh missionaries brought the Gospel to us in 1910, and since then, all Paites are Christians—at least nominally.

women and some even had children (Ezra 10:44b), and we have no account of the situation of the *golah* community or of the foreign wives after that. At least it can be said that such actions were not repeated, or at least not attested in the Bible, neither in the Old Testament nor the New Testament. Even Nehemiah did not send away even though he used physical violence to object and admonish such intermarriages (Neh 13:23–28). Furthermore, interpreting it as a "mass divorce" might not have been the case since it seems to affect a small percentage of the community—about 111 people out of about 30,000 returned exiles; 0.58 percent of the clergy and about 0.67 percent of the lay people.[2] It is important to study the whole narrative to understand the whole picture.

Certainly, difficult texts like Ezra should be read and engaged with, not quickly dismissed or even judged as "negative." But with diligence and creativity, and prayerfully, they should be studied before implementing them into our own contexts. The *golah* community themselves were trying to apply the Scripture ("law") in their context (as seen in the prayer of Ezra [Ezra 9] and in the proposal made by Shecaniah [Ezra 10:3]). Yet, claiming and accepting the authority of the Scripture does not necessarily imply only one way interpretation and application for our situations today. Not all texts in the canon are meant to be imperative, some are indicative, as Ezra would be.[3] As such, the best we can do is to engage with the text, wholly and faithfully. We obviously need better and concrete ways to relate with the "other" in our context, in the Paite tribal Christian context and in the larger global Christian context. What that means, however, is beyond the scope of this work and would require another project.

---

2. Klein, *Ezra & Nehemiah*, 745–46; Shepherd and Wright, *Ezra and Nehemiah*, 149.
3. Shepherd and Wright, *Ezra and Nehemiah*, 150.

Appendix 1

People/s of the Land/s

IN THE BOOK OF Ezra, the phrase appears in both the plural form and the singular form. In the plural, it appears in two forms—the peoples of the lands (Ezra 3:3; 9:1-2, 11) and the peoples of the land (Ezra 10:2, 11), and in the singular as people of the land (Ezra 4:4). While no specific identifications are provided, the phrases are clearly used in reference to "other" people, not the *golah* community, for whom the identifications are clear, the main terms being "*golah*" and "Israel." And the terms being vaguely used, the variations in the plural form would simply be variants in the term and not a way to refer to different groups of people.[1] The different forms of the phrase will be discussed below, starting with the plural forms.

Peoples of the Land/s
(Ezra 3:3; 9:1-2, 11; 10:2, 11)

The phrase in plural appears in two different forms in the book of Ezra: peoples of the land (Ezra 10:2, 11) and peoples of the lands (Ezra 3:3; 9:1, 2, 11). While no specific identifications are provided, the contexts are clear that the phrases are used in reference to "other" people, not the *golah* community. The variations in the plural form would simply be variants in the term and not a way to refer to different groups of people.

---

1. The variant forms could be an indication of two separate authors, but would still refer to the same people. See Fried, *Ezra*, 392.

APPENDIX 1

Peoples of the Lands (*'ammê hāărāṣôt*)

In Ezra 3:3, the *golah* group who have returned from the Babylonian exile to Judah are afraid of these peoples of the lands. There is no further information for specific identification for the peoples of the lands, of whom the *golah* people are afraid of. It does, however, indicate that there were other, non-*golah* people, in or around the land when they returned. The only clue in the context is that these peoples of the lands would be those who are not worshipping YHWH, or at least not in the way of the *golah* people.

Even though it is not said whether the *golah* who returned to the land settled in the land with ease or faced difficulties (Ezra 2:70), it can be assumed that they might have had some struggles. The *golah* returnees could have struggled to fit back in the land, trying to find homes and lands, while those who had been dwelling there might not have been so willing to give up their homes and lands to the new arrivals. Naturally, they would also have struggled to resettle back into the land culturally and cultically. For instance, the *golah* returnees are building an altar "according to the law of Moses" (Ezra 3:2), and they start observing festival and burnt offerings "as prescribed" (Ezra 3:4). Possibly, the cultic ways of the newly arrived *golah* people might be different from that of those who have been dwelling in the land. And these struggles and differences could have resulted in a feeling of insecurity or dread in the "new-comers"—the *golah* returnees. Also, Ezra 3:3 states that the altar was built "in its original site." It could be that the *golah* group was building a new altar by destroying the one that existed until the *golah* returns, which would have consequently upset those who have been there and using the altar.[2] The text also states that the *golah* group is observing the Tabernacles "as is written" and offering the burnt offerings "as is prescribed" (Ezra 3:4). Thus, how the *golah* group are now carrying out these cultic activities "according to the law of Moses" and "as is written and prescribed" might be different from how the existing inhabitants did. Most of all, what the context discloses is that, the peoples of the lands are not the *golah* people. They could be any non-*golah* people, either non-exiled Jews or non-Jews or both, who were dwelling in the land when the *golah* returned to the land.

Secondly, the phrase peoples of the lands also appear in Ezra 9:1–2, 11. In Ezra 9:1–2, the phrase is used in a report to Ezra how the *golah*

---

2. Fensham, *Books of Ezra and Nehemiah*, 59. There are also other scholars who reason similarly. For example, see Fleishman, "Echo of Optimism," 14.

community failed to keep themselves apart from the peoples of the lands resulting in the mixing of the holy seed with the peoples of the lands. In Ezra 9:11, it is said that the land that the Israelites were entering was filled with the uncleanness of the peoples of the lands. The phrase "peoples of the lands" (Ezra 9:11) appears to refer to the people who lived in the land before the Israelites conquered it. So it is unclear whether the same phrase in Ezra 9:11 and in 9:2, where it refers to their contemporaries, are used in different ways. But, it must be noted that this mention in Ezra 9:11 is made within the prayer of Ezra quoting commandments. Furthermore, in the book of Ezra, all or any non-*golah* people tend to be treated together into one broad "other" group.[3] The one piece of information the text does provide about the "other" people is their enumeration in a list with other people who have abominations like (*kĕ*) those of the Canaanites, Hittites, Perizzites, Jebusites, Ammonites, Moabites, Egyptians, and Amorites (Ezra 9:1, 11). Such a characterization itself does not however specifically identify the "others" because they are simply likened to the actions of some nations of the past. In fact, there is no exact source of these nations appearing together in the Hebrew Bible.[4] Evidently, this listing of nations is random and serves more to stereotype rather than reference specific nations.

Thus, while the peoples of the lands in Ezra 9:1 and 9:11 are referencing to different periods of time, the phrase still means the same kinds of people. What is common between these two appearances of the phrase is that both peoples referred to have abominations which are not acceptable for the *golah* people. Thus, following the above points, the same phrase in Ezra 9:1–2 and in 9:11 are not necessarily inconsistent and they will refer to the same (broad) group of non-*golah* people, from whom the *golah* people have to remain apart.

---

3. Peoples of the lands (Ezra 3:3), adversaries of Judah and Benjamin (4:1), people of the land (4:4), peoples of the lands (9:1, 2), peoples of the land (10:2, 11), foreign women (10:2, 10–11, 14).

4. As Williamson concludes, the first four and last nations in the list (Canaanites, Hittites, Preizzites, Jebusites, Amorites) could have come from Deut 7:1, nations with whom intermarriage is prohibited for fear of apostasy (Deut 7:3–4). The other two nations (Ammonites and Moabites) could have come from Deut 23:4, and referred to those who should not be admitted into their assembly. See Williamson, *Ezra, Nehemiah*, 131.

Appendix 1

Peoples of the Land (*'ammê hāʾăreṣ*)

Thirdly, the phrase in the plural appears in a variant form, peoples of the land in Ezra 10:2 and 10:11. The form is best to be understood as a variant of the plural form discussed above, peoples of the lands, carrying the same meaning.

Ezra 10 narrates the response of the people to the situation that is narrated in Ezra 9. After the people came to realize their unfaithfulness of not keeping themselves apart from "other" people and intermarrying with foreign women, a proposal was made to resolve the situation they ran into. In Ezra 10:2 Shecaniah reports to Ezra that the *golah* people have married women from the peoples of the land, but how there is still hope to redeem themselves from their situation. The proposal is that they would make a covenant with God to send away all their foreign wives and the children born from the foreign wives. Later, Ezra exhorts the people to make confession to God and to keep themselves apart from the peoples of the land (Ezra 10:11). Some argue that the peoples of the land are simply those Jews who did not go into exile, thereby the issue would be inner-Yehudite conflicts.[5] On the other hand, there are others who argue that there is no evidence of inter-Yehudite conflicts.[6] In response to these two opposing views, the text remains vague when it comes to identification of the peoples of the land except characterize them as people from whom the *golah* community should remain apart. As such, the peoples of the land could be anyone, any group of people other than the *golah* group—non-exiled Jews or non-Israelites—who lived such lifestyles as those stereotyped nations and are unacceptable to the *golah* community.

Outside of the book of Ezra, the phrase peoples of the land/s in other appearances in the Hebrew Bible also often refers to non-Israelites and non-Yahwists. In most cases, the term peoples of the land/s refers to people in the general sense: those people who worship other gods, in contrast to those who worship YHWH; or to identify other gods (of the peoples of the land) in contrast to YHWH (the God of Israel/Jews). For example, in Josh 4:24, the phrase peoples of the land refers to the peoples whom Israelites encountered on their way to Canaan. No one specific group is singled out, simply non-Israelites in general who had not yet known about YHWH.

---

5. See, for instance, Becking, "On the Identity of the 'Foreign' Women," 31–43; Williamson, "Welcome Home," 113–23.

6. See, for instance, Oded, "Time of Zerubbabel," 265; Becking, "On the Identity of the 'Foreign Women," 34–42; Japhet, "People and Land," 104.

People/s of the Land/s

In Esth 8:17, the phrase peoples of the land refers to different peoples of different provinces in the Persian Empire. These peoples from different provinces were worshippers of other gods. Other appearances of the phrase in this form include: peoples of the land (Zeph 3:20; Deut 28:10; 1 Kgs 8:43; 53; 1 Chr 5:25; 6:33; Ezek 31:12) and peoples of the lands (2 Chr 13:9; 32:13). In these appearances as well, the common implication is that they refer to non-Israelites/Jews, non-YHWH worshippers, but with no clear specificity of which group they belong to.

Scholars such as Lisbeth Fried also assert that the phrase in this plural form, peoples of the land mostly refers to non-Judeans/non-Israelites (Esth 8:17; Ezek 31:12; Zeph 3:20; 2 Chr 32:13).[7] Fried further claims that the phrase (in the plural) has the same meaning in all appearances in the Hebrew Bible: "The authors of Ezra-Nehemiah, and the author of Ezra 3:3, use the plural forms of the term in the same way that all biblical authors have used them. There is no indication anywhere that the authors of Ezra-Nehemiah, or of Ezra 3:3, employed a meaning different to that of other biblical writers."[8] In Fried's reasoning, however, these peoples are those who later became the Persian satrapies of Egypt, Cilicia and Beyond the River. That is, the phrase refers to the "the peoples of the neighboring provinces" and their leaders the governors of these provinces, which is also how it is used in Ezra.[9] For Fried, then, the phrase refers to the Persian officials whom the *golah* community were afraid of earlier in the narrative (Ezra 3:3), but are the ones whom they had intermarried with by the time of Ezra's return (Ezra 9:2, 11).[10]

In response to Fried, I agree that the phrase refers to non-*golah* people and that it means the same kind of people in all appearances. In assigning specific, distinct identification, however, my findings have indicated otherwise. There is not enough evidence to specifically identify the peoples of the land in the book of Ezra with the Persian officials, or any other specific distinctive group. Particularly, the intermarriage of the *golah* people that the text is most concerned about with the foreign women (Ezra 9:2; 10:2, 10–11, 14, 17, 19). It is unlikely that there would be many Persian officials

---

7. Fried also argues that the phrase in this form appears only in the exilic and postexilic texts, and out of the 24 occurrences in the plural form, 16 are in Ezra, Nehemiah, and Chronicles. See Fried, "Because of the Dread," 458.

8. Fried, "Because of the Dread," 459.

9. Fried, "Because of the Dread," 469.

10. Fried, *Ezra*, 362, 382–83.

Appendix 1

who were women, or that all the foreign women whom the *golah* men married would be Persian officials. As Fried herself notes, in Ezra (and Nehemiah) it is not usually clear who the phrase is referring to, except that the nations they are likened to are peoples with whom the Israelites shared the land of Canaan at the time of settlement (Ezra 9:1).[11] In addition, while the argument that the phrase references the peoples in the neighboring provinces should not be ruled out, there is no evidence that the phrase could not also include people within the province of Yehud itself. Also, in regard to the fear of the peoples of the lands in Ezra 3:3, while it is not impossible that the *golah* returnees would have had some kind of fear of the governors of the neighboring provinces, it is also quite possible that, as recently returned and "new" back in the land, they would be in dread of the general populace. In fact, in the book of Ezra, the Persians are usually named—as kings Cyrus (Ezra 1:1–2, 7; 4:5), Darius (4:5; 5:5, 7; 6:1), Ahasuerus (4:6), Artaxerxes (4:7), and officials such as Bishlam, Mithredath, Tabeel (4:7), Rehum, Shimshai and colleagues (4:8, 9, 17), Tattenai, Shethar-bozenai and colleagues (5:3; 6:6, 13). Except for these named Persian officials (and Sidonians and Tyrians [Ezra 3:7]), the book of Ezra tends to leave identification of non-*golah* people vague, as already discussed.

From the foregoing discussion it can be concluded that the phrase, in the plural form (peoples of the land/s), refers to non-Israelites/non-Judeans (foreigners), that is, non-*golah* people, and that non-*golah* people would encompass all or any who are not a part of the *golah* community. Non-exiled Jews are not mentioned in the narrative, and they seem to be lumped together with all "other" people. The same meaning applies to the singular form of the phrase, as we will see below.

People of the Land (*'am hā'ăreṣ*)

In the book of Ezra, the phrase in the singular, people of the land, is also used in a vague sense, thereby not allowing specific identification. The phrase people of the land is best understood as a broad term referring to any non-*golah*, non-exiled Jews or non-Jews.

In Ezra 4, the *golah* people have commenced the building of the temple, but then soon faced obstruction from other people, designated as people of the land in Ezra 4:4. The phrase people of the land is juxtaposed with the phrase people of Judah who would refer to the protagonist group

---

11. Fried, "Because of the Dread," 458.

of the narrative, the *golah* people. This juxtapositioning indicates a differentiation of the people of the land from the *golah* people, and they indeed were the ones creating trouble and halting the prominent project of the *golah* people, to build the temple. Described as simply people of the land with no further helpful clue for specific identification and juxtaposed with the *golah* people as the people of Judah, it is if they were living in Judah as usurpers. A similar reasoning has been seen earlier in the narrative as well. In the *golah* list of Ezra 2, when the names of the returnees are listed according to their domicile (instead of fathers' names), there is no question of the genealogy of those from the region of Judah and Benjamin (Ezra 2:20–35). But, for those from Babylon, their Israelite descent is questioned (Ezra 2:59–60). It appears that there is a possible correlation between being of/from "Judah" and truly worshipping YHWH and similarly, not being of/from Judah with not truly worshipping YHWH. This implies that the people of the land are those who were in the land of Judah when the *golah* arrived and though they might have worshipped YHWH, it was different from the Yahwistic ways of the *golah* group.[12] As such, the text suggests that they may not be connected or associated with the land of Judah, even though they would be living on the land of Judah and surrounding areas.

The immediate context of Ezra 4:4 and the larger context of how non-*golah* people are being referenced, also calls for understanding the phrase people of the land as open to refer to any officials and general populace, or both foreigners and non-exiled Jews, who were not part of the *golah* community and their project. In John Tracy Thames words, the phrase would include "'everyone in a particular locality who is relevant to a particular set of circumstances,' but with the deliberate intent to efface or obfuscate the exact actor(s)."[13] That is, the phrase as it is used in Ezra 4:4 is not inter-

---

12. As Dalit Rom-Shiloni points out, it appears that Ezra (and Nehemiah) is not the only literature narrating the existence of such "adversarial," YHWH-worshipping communities in post-exilic Judah. For instance, other exilic texts such as Ezekiel (Ezek 11:15–21; 33:23–29) indicate opposing Yahwistic communities. See Rom-Shiloni, "From Ezekiel to Ezra-Nehemiah," 129.

Similarly, Sara Japhet also identifies three Yahwistic communities in the land of Israel—the community of "returned exiles" which settled in Judah and Jerusalem (Ezra 2:1; 3:8; 6:21, and so on), another group that comprises the inhabitants of Judah who were not exiled at all and remained in the land, and a third group of the Israelite habitants of northern Israel who remained in Samaria and Galilee after the Assyrian conquest; and two more communities outside the land of Israel—the community of Judean exiles which settled in Babylonia and later also in Persia, and the community of Judeans in Egypt. See Japhet, "People and Land," 104.

13. Thames, "New Discussion," 120.

ested in the exact identity of the people but rather puts emphasis on their action of obstructing the *golah* people's work, and also it provides a contrast between the important and unimportant characters.[14] The whole chapter of Ezra 4 deals with the obstructions the *golah* community people faced in their building projects, and in the whole book of Ezra, the non-*golah* people tend to be identified vaguely and all non-*golah* people tend to be treated together in a broad group. Such usages seem to suit very well the usage of the term people of the land (as well as in its plural form, peoples of the land/s) in the book of Ezra. Ultimately, the characterization of the people of the land serves to characterize the *golah* people.

On the other hand, Fried argues that the phrase people of the land always refers to the landed "aristocracy, the elites who control and administer an area."[15] She reasons so because they were able to bribe the Persian officials to disrupt the building work of the *golah* community, and as such they would be the Persian satrapal officials.[16] In response to Fried, from the current context and the use of different and rather vague terms for "other" people in the book of Ezra, it is difficult to say whether the phrase the people of the land (Ezra 4:4) could be specifically identified. Furthermore, as Thames also notes, there is no indication in the text about the kind of bribery, monetary, economic or what means, was involved or what the officials actually did to trouble the building work of the *golah*.[17] At best, the people of the land comprises a broad group encompassing any or all non-*golah* people, who are not part of the *golah* group and in fact obstructing the work of the *golah*.

In the larger context of the Hebrew Bible, the usage of the phrase people of the land has generally been understood in two main trajectories over the history of interpretation. One is to take it as a technical term to mean a representative, land-owning, leadership, small group of people, who also are rich and influential both politically and economically in the society; The other is to interpret the phrase literally, as referring to ordinary people, the populace in general.[18] On the other hand, the phrase has also been

---

14. Thames, "New Discussion," 125.
15. Fried, "Because of the Dread," 458. See also Fried, "'am ha'ares in Ezra 4:4," 125.
16. Fried, "'am ha'ares in Ezra 4:4," 130.
17. Thames, "New Discussion," 117.
18. John Tracy Thames traces the different interpretations of the phrase from the early twentieth century. Traditionally, the phrase seems to be understood as a technical term for a leadership group of some sort: for representative government in ancient Israel (Mayer Sulzberger), "the landed gentry, the landowners, the landed aristocracy, the lords

explained as having different meanings according to the time period. For instance, for the pre-exilic era it is generally understood to comprise the class of free, landowning, full citizens of preexilic Judah, but its meaning has changed over the period of the exile and in the postexilic era such a technical definition of the term changed from a clearly defined stratum of the free Yahwistic society determined to retain their religious and political freedom to the common people who, unlike the preexilic people of the land, were no longer diligent in their duties and observant of their religion.[19] With such a wide and diversified treatment of the phrase by scholars, it calls for a brief re-examination of the appearances. An examination of several of the appearances of the phrase throughout the Hebrew Bible indicates that the phrase does not necessarily carry one meaning in all cases.

In many texts the phrase people of the land does not refer to leaders, landed aristocrats or the poor. For instance, the phrase is used to refer to Israelites or Judeans as cultic people or a political group of people (2 Kgs 15:5; Lev 4:27; 20:2; Ezek 45:22). And in other references, it is used to refer to foreign peoples (Gen 23:7, Hittites; Exod 5:5, Egyptians; Num 14:9, Canaanites). In Lev 4:27, the phrase must refer to ordinary people, just after listing rulers and priests in 4:22–26. Leviticus 20:2 would also be referring to people in general, making comparisons with aliens. Ezekiel 45:22 refers to the participants in the Passover, which would include common people and not just cultic officials. Jeremiah 34:19 would also refer to general people, just after listing officials of Judah and Jerusalem, eunuchs and priests, with whom the king makes a covenant. Genesis 42:6 would refer to all people to whom Joseph sold food, Egyptians and non-Egyptians, including Israelites.[20] Exodus 5:5 would refer to the Egyptians in general.

---

of the land, the representatives of the people" (Samuel Daiches), a politically and militarily preeminent group (Ernst Würthwein).

Later, there were other arguments to interpret it not as a technical term but referring to a very general manner varying from context to context (Ernest W. Nicholson), or that it can be used in two ways—to refer to the entirety of any particular group of people, or, as a technical term that designated a particular Judean political group (Shemaryahu Talmon), or that it "comprised the class of free, landowning, full citizens of preexilic Judah" (Lisbeth Fried).

Thames argues that the phrase should be read as a literary expression for something very ordinary, an idiomatic expression for "everyone in a particular locality who is relevant to a particular set of circumstances, but with the deliberate intent to efface or obfuscate the exact actor(s)" (Thames, "New Discussion," 110–20).

19. Coggins, "Interpretation of Ezra 4:4," 125.

20. Fried argues that if Joseph was selling to all peoples in general he would have

Appendix 1

In many of its appearances in Kings there also is no strong reason why the phrase could not refer to general people/subjects. 2 Kings 25:3 expresses that there is no food to eat for the people of the land because of severe famine, thus it refers to the general people. In 2 Kgs 11:14 (cf. 2 Chr 23:13), chiefs or officials are already listed, so it seems that the phrase does not rule out the implication to mean general people (see also 2 Chr 23:20).

In some other occurrences the phrase is ambiguous and can refer either the general people or leaders. For instance, in 2 Kgs 15:5 the king's son (Jotham) is ruling over the people of the land in place of his father (Azariah). The phrase could technically mean the ministers of the king upon whom the king directly rules, but the possibility of interpreting it to mean ruling over the general populace cannot be completely ruled out. In Num 14:9, it could refer mainly to the ruling, upper class Canaanites, yet it could still be understood as all Canaanites of whom the Israelites should not be afraid. Of course, in some references, the contexts are clear that the phrase refers to the ruling or upper class people. For instance, in 2 Kgs 21:24 the people of the land who made Josiah king in place of his father king Amon, would be those who have some leadership role. Also in 2 Kgs 23:30, when Josiah died, the people of the land who made his son Jehoahaz king would be people with power or authority to anoint the king. In 2 Kgs 16:15, where the priest makes offerings for the king and the people of the land, it refers to the king and his representatives. The above short survey of the occurrences of the phrase people of the land then reveals that the phrase does not carry one fixed meaning across all occurrences and it is most crucial is to study the context in order to understand the meaning of the phrase.

---

sold "to the heads of the landed estates in Egypt," but her argument lacks enough solid support, though she cites herself in regard to distributory roles of large estates in Egypt. See Fried, "'am ha'ares in Ezra 4:4," 126.

Appendix 2

The Law of YHWH/God/Moses

There is no concrete definition in the Bible for the torah, normally translated into English as "law" or "teaching." There is, however, a general conception and expectation that obeying the law is obedience to God and breaking the law is disobedience to YHWH.[1] Also, different terms are used to refer to the torah—such as "book of Moses" (Neh 13:1), "the book of the Law" (2 Kgs 22:8), "the book of the law of Moses" (2 Kgs 14:6; Neh 8:1), "the book of the law of God" (Neh 8:8), "the book of YHWH given through Moses" (2 Chr 34:14), and such.[2] In the most general terms, then, torah or "law" can be understood as a set of regulations or guidelines that the people are expected to follow to be the people of YHWH.

Law plays a central role in the book of Ezra. However, specific identification of the "law" is not usually provided and various terminologies are used to refer to it. Could the "law" in Ezra be referring to the Pentateuch generally or just to the legal portions of the Pentateuch? Or, could the "law" be referring only to the Deuteronomic laws? Varied terms are used to refer to the law in Ezra including torah of Moses or of YHWH or God, book of Moses, law (Aramaic), scroll of torah, words of the torah. It is also not clear in what form the community in Ezra had the "law." The use of the term scroll implies that it must have been a written text, yet torah itself can simply be a non-codified set of rules and not necessarily a written-text.[3] In the book of Ezra, as different terms and descriptions are used for the "law" that

---

1. Japhet, "Law and 'The Law,'" 99.
2. Japhet, "Law and 'The Law,'" 99–100.
3. Becking, "Law as Expression of Religion," 22.

the community should obey, it is best to understand the "law" in general terms. In Becking's words, the concept of "law" in the book of Ezra is not so much a rigid-law in the strictest sense, but more like a viable symbol, a reference to set standards for the life of the community in relation to YHWH.[4] The different terms for "law" employed in the book of Ezra are as follows:

Torah of Moses (*tôrâ*): The first group of *golah* who returned to Jerusalem made altar and offered burnt offerings according to the torah of Moses (Ezra 3:2) and celebrated the festival of Tabernacle and fulfilled daily burnt offerings as is written and prescribed (Ezra 3:4). Later, Ezra is introduced as a scribe skilled in the torah of Moses (Ezra 7:6). In Neh 8, which is also part of Ezra tradition, Ezra was asked by the people to read from the torah of Moses (Neh 8:1).

Scroll of Moses (Aramaic, *sĕpar*): As the temple rebuilding was finished, priests and Levites are appointed for their services in the temple, as it is written in the scroll of Moses (Ezra 6:18).

Torah of YHWH: Ezra is described as someone who dedicated himself to the study of the torah of YHWH, and he is also to observe and teach it to Israel (Ezra 7:10).

Scroll of the Torah of God: The Levites were reading from the scroll of the torah of God (Neh 8:8). Ezra is described as reading from the scroll of the torah of God (Neh 8:18).

The (words of the) Torah: In response to the request from the people to read them the torah of Moses (Neh 8:1), Ezra brought the torah before them (Neh 8:2). The Levites explained the torah to the people (Neh 8:7), and the people were weeping as they listened to the words of the torah (Neh 8:9). On the second day of the Sukkoth festival, the leaders of people, the priests and the Levites gathered before Ezra to study the words of the torah (Neh 8:13). As they studied, they found in the torah that they should dwell in booths during the Sukkoth festival (Neh 8:14–15), and they did so (8:16–17).

Law of God (Aramaic, *dāt*): In Artaxerxes's letter of commission to Ezra, Ezra is a scribe in the law of the God of heaven (Ezra 7:12) who was sent to lead Judah and Jerusalem according to the law of God (Ezra 7:14). Artaxerxes also ordered that whatever Ezra the priest and scribe in the law of the God of heaven requested should be dispatched (Ezra 7:21). Ezra was commissioned to appoint judges who knew the laws of God as well as teach

---

4. Becking, "Law as Expression of Religion," 22.

The Law of YHWH/God/Moses

those who did not know them (Ezra 7:25). Finally, Artaxerxes warned that those who did not obey the law of God should be punished (Ezra 7:26).

From the list above, it can be seen that there are various references to the "law" in the book of Ezra. From the contexts in which these varying terms are used, however, it can be seen that they refer to be general "law" or "law book." The torah of Moses, the torah of YHWH or simply the torah seem to be used interchangeably. For instance, within Ezra 7 itself Ezra is described as a scribe in the torah of Moses (7:6) and also someone dedicated to the study of the torah of YHWH (7:10). There are also no contradictory points in these "laws." The "law" seems to be the Pentateuch in general although perhaps not in the exact canonical form as we have it.

An important question is whether the Persians be so interested in validating the torah, or could Artaxerxes's commission instead be Persian rules and laws? Judging from the context, the "law" used when Ezra deals with the *golah* community back in Jerusalem is clearly the torah and not some foreign Persian law.[5] Ezra is someone dedicated to study the torah and he was commissioned to teach its stipulations to Israel (Ezra 7:10). Artaxerxes king of Persia commissioned him to judge Judah and Jerusalem according to the law of his (Ezra's) God which was in his (Ezra's) hand (Ezra 7:14). These statements imply that the law must be the torah that Ezra already has, not a new one. The text also presents the Persian kings as very supportive of the *golah* community; Cyrus himself was stirred by YHWH to issue the edict for the *golah* people to return and rebuild the temple in Jerusalem (Ezra 1:1–4). Furthermore, the Persians are known to be tolerant of their subjects worshipping their own deity and following local laws. Thus, there is no reason to doubt that the Persians would allow and even appoint Ezra to teach his people according to their own law. The "law" that Ezra brought with him, and the "law" in general in the whole narrative will not be Persian law, but the Pentateuch in some form.

Truly, there are no direct quotations from the Pentateuch that are referenced in Ezra. For instance, when Ezra quotes the "law" in his prayer about how the people broke (YHWH's) commandment (Ezra 9:11–12), the quotations could have come from different parts of the "law" such as: "The land which you are entering to possess" (Deut 7:1); "A land unclean by the uncleanness of the peoples of the lands" (Lev 18:27); "By their abominations" (Deut 18:12); "Do not give your daughters" (Deut 7:3); "Do not seek

---

5. As also argued in Grabbe, *Ezra-Nehemiah*, 144–45.

Appendix 2

their well being and prosperity" (Deut 23:7); and so on.[6] It seems that Ezra collects different stipulations from the Pentateuch to describe the situation they were in. Other references to the law in Ezra can also be connected generally to the Pentateuch. For instance: the Tabernacle festival in Ezra 3:4 and Neh 8:14–17 can be more or less connected with Lev 23:33–36; the Passover and Unleavened Bread celebration in Ezra 6:19–22 with Lev 23:5–8 and Deut 16:1–8; Ezra 9:1–2 with Deut 7:3.[7] That Ezra might have had a law book different from the Pentateuch is unlikely.

Long before Ezra came to Jerusalem, the first group of returnees had already fulfilled the law—for instance, offering burnt offerings and festival observed according to the law (Ezra 3:2, 4), and appointing priests and Levites according to the law when the temple was completed (Ezra 6:18) and Passover and festival celebrated (Ezra 6:19–22). That is, they had the "law" in some ways—whether in written form or memorized—they had some kind of access. Perhaps the people had become lenient in observing the law that Ezra on his arrival had to lead the people to reenact cultic activities according to the law (Neh 8:14–17). There are no signs that the law the people had before and after the arrival of Ezra are contradictory or different. As such, the law that the people had been observing and the law Ezra brought and implemented must be broadly the same. Thus, in the book of Ezra (including Neh 8) the torah of YHWH/Moses/God and *dāt* refer to the same thing, which can be broadly identified as the Pentateuch.

Beyond understanding the laws in Ezra as broadly the Pentateuchal laws, it remains open which "law" is being referred to, and at times there are no known laws to address the issue. For instance, in dealing with the intermarriage with foreign women, the proposed solution is to send away the foreign wives and their children (Ezra 10:3); however, there is no known Pentateuchal law demanding such an action. Furthermore, claims such as intermarriage as the cause of the exile, of being under foreign subjugation, being given to the sword, to humiliation and that continuing intermarriage would lead to no remnant (Ezra 9:7, 14) are to be understood as interpretations of the "law," as there are no laws stating such correlations. There is no Pentateuchal law prohibiting intermarriage in general. In Exod 34:11–16 and Deut 7:1–3, there are warnings not to intermarry with the Canaanite nations, but not foreign nations in general, which seems to be the case in Ezra 9–10. The people themselves seem confused about how to handle the

---

6. Blenkinsopp, *Ezra-Nehemiah*, 185.
7. Grabbe, *Ezra-Nehemiah*, 146.

unprecedented situation they faced and they turned to Ezra for advice such that the solution proposed would also be in accordance to their counsel (Ezra 10:1–3). Thus, the Pentateuchal law was being interpreted in order to address the situation they faced.

The "law" that is referred to in the narrative of Ezra can be understood as the Pentateuch, but it cannot be expected that the references are exactly to the Pentateuch as we have it now.[8] An author in antiquity may not have been so keen in exact citations, or that the Pentateuch available to the author was not necessarily in the same form as what we have now.

---

8. For more discussion on the law in Ezra, see Williamson, *Ezra, Nehemiah*, xxxvii–xxxix; Grabbe, *Ezra-Nehemiah*, 143–50; Blenkinsopp, *Ezra-Nehemiah*, 152–57; Japhet, "Law and 'The Law.'"

Bibliography

Arnold, Bill T. "The Use of Aramaic in the Hebrew Bible: Another Look at Biligualism in Ezra and Daniel." *JNSL* 22 (1996) 1–16.

Bakon, Shimon. "The Mystery of the Urim ve-Thummim." *JBQ* 43 (2015) 241–45.

Batten, Loring W. *A Critical and Exegetical Commentary on the Books of Ezra and Nehemiah*. International Critical Commentary. Edinburgh: T. & T. Clark, 1913.

Becking, Bob. "Continuity and Community: The Belief System of the Book of Ezra." In *Crisis of Israelite Religion: Transformation of Religious Tradition in Exilic and Postexilic Times*, edited by Bob Becking, et al., 256–75. Oudtestamentische Studiën 42. Leiden: Brill, 1999.

———. "Law as Expression of Religion (Ezra 7–10)." In *Yahwism after the Exile: Perspectives on Israelite Religion in the Persian Ezra*, edited by Rainer Albertz, et al., 18–31. Studies in Theology and Religion. Assen: Royal Van Gorcum, 2003.

———. "On the Identity of the 'Foreign Women' in Ezra 9–10." In *Exile and Restoration Revisited: Essays on the Babylonian and Persian Periods in Memory of Peter R. Ackroyd*, edited by Gary N. Knoppers, et al., 31–49. London: T. & T. Clark, 2009.

Bedford, Peter Ross. *Temple Restoration in Early Achaemenid Judah*. Journal for the Study of Judaism Supplements 65. Leiden: Brill, 2001.

Ben-Zvi, Ehud. "Inclusion in and Exclusion from Israel as Conveyed by the Use of the Term 'Israel' in Post-Monarchic Biblical Texts." In *The Pitcher Is Broken: Memorial Essays for Gösta W. Ahlstrom*, edited by Steven W. Holloway, et al., 95–149. JSOTSup 190. Sheffield: Sheffield Academic, 1995.

Berman, Joshua. "The Narratological Purpose of Aramaic Prose in Ezra 4.8–6.18." *Aramaic Studies* 5 (2007) 165–91. https://doi.org/10.1163/147783507X252658.

Berquist, Jon. "Construction of Identity in Postcolonial Yehud." In *Judah and Judeans in the Persian Period*, edited by Oded Lipchits, et al., 53–66. Winona Lake, IN: Eisenbrauns, 2006.

Blenkinsopp, Joseph. *Ezra-Nehemiah: A Commentary*. OTL. Philadelphia: Westminster, 1988.

———. *Judaism, the First Phase: The Place of Ezra and Nehemiah in the Origins of Judaism*. Grand Rapids: Eerdmans, 2009.

Botterweck, G. Johannes, and Helmer Ringgren. *Theological Dictionary of the Old Testament*. Grand Rapids: Eerdmans, 1974.

Brown, A. Philip, II. "The Problem of Mixed Marriages in Ezra 9–10." *BSac* 162.648 (2005) 437–58.

Bibliography

Brown, Francis, et al. *The Brown, Driver, Briggs Hebrew and English Lexicon: With an Appendix Containing the Biblical Aramaic: Coded with the Numbering System from Strong's Exhaustive Concordance of the Bible.* Thirteenth Printing. Peabody: Hendrickson, 2010.

Causse, Antonin. "From an Ethnic Group to a Religious Community: The Sociological Problem of Judaism." In *Community, Identity, and Ideology: Social Science Approaches to the Hebrew Bible*, edited by Charles E. Carter, et al., 95–118. Winona Lake, IN: Eisenbrauns, 1996.

Childs, Brevard S. *The Book of Exodus: A Critical, Theological Commentary.* OTL. Philadelphia: Westminster, 1974.

———. *Introduction to the Old Testament as Scripture.* Philadelphia: Fortress, 1979.

———. *Isaiah.* OTL. Louisville: Westminster John Knox, 2001.

Choi, John H. *Traditions at Odds: The Reception of the Pentateuch in Biblical and Second Temple Period Literature.* LHBOTS 518. New York: T. & T. Clark, 2010.

Clauss, John. "Understanding the Mixed Marriages of Ezra-Nehemiah in the Light of Temple-Building and the Book's Concept of Jerusalem." In *Mixed Marriages: Intermarriage and Group Identity in the Second Temple Period*, edited by Christian Frevel, 109–31. LHBOTS 540. New York: T. & T. Clark, 2011.

Clines, David J. A. "Alleged Basic Meanings of the Hebrew Verb *Qdš* 'Be Holy': An Exercise in Comparative Hebrew Lexicography." https://www.academia.edu/28065748/Alleged_Basic_Meanings_of_the_Hebrew_Verb_qd%C5%A1_be_holy_An_Exercise_in_Comparative_Hebrew_Lexicography.

———. *The Dictionary of Classical Hebrew.* 9 vols. Sheffield: Sheffield Academic, 1993–2012.

———. *Ezra, Nehemiah, Esther: Based on the Revised Standard Version.* New Century Bible Commentary. Grand Rapids: Eerdmans, 1984.

Cogan, Mordechai. "For We, Like You, Worship Your God: Three Biblical Portrayals of Samaritan Origins." *VT* 38 (1988) 286–92.

Coggins, Richard. J. "Interpretation of Ezra 4:4." *JTS* 16 (1965) 124–27.

———. *Samaritans and Jews: The Origins of Samaritanism Reconsidered.* Growing Points in Theology. Oxford: Black-well, 1975.

Dor, Yonina. "The Rite of Separation of the Foreign Wives in Ezra-Nehemiah." In *Judah and the Judeans in the Achaemenid Period: Negotiating Identity in an International Context*, edited by Oded Lipschits, et al., 173–88. Winona Lake, IN: Eisenbrauns, 2011.

Erbele-Küster, Dorothea. *Body, Gender, and Purity in Leviticus 12 and 15.* LHBOTS 539. London: Bloomsbury T. & T. Clark, 2017.

Eskenazi, Tamara Cohn. "Imagining the Other and Constructing Israelite Identity in Ezra-Nehemiah." In *Imagining the Other and Constructing Israelite Identity in the Early Second Temple Period*, edited by Ehud Ben Zvi, et al., 230–56. LHBOTS 456. New York: Bloomsbury T. & T. Clark, 2014.

———. *In an Age of Prose: A Literary Approach to Ezra-Nehemiah.* Atlanta: Scholars, 1988.

Eskenazi, Tamara Cohn, and Eleanore P. Judd. "Marriage to a Stranger in Ezra 9–10." In *Second Temple Studies 2: Temple Community in the Persian Period*, edited by Tamara C. Eskenazi and Kent H. Richards, 266–85. JSOTSup 175. Sheffield: Sheffield Academic, 1994.

Bibliography

Esler, Philip F. "Ezra-Nehemiah as a Narrative of (Re-invented) Israelite Identity." *BibInt* 11 (2003) 413-26.

Fensham, F. Charles. *The Books of Ezra and Nehemiah*. Grand Rapids: Eerdmans, 1982.

Finkelstein, Israel. "Saul, Benjamin and the Emergence of 'Biblical Israel': An Alternative View." *ZAW* 123 (2011) 348-67. https://doi.org/10.1515/ZAW.2011.024.

Fleishman, Joseph. "An Echo of Optimism in Ezra 6:19-22." *HUCA* 69 (1998) 15-29.

Fried, Lisbeth S. "The 'am Hā'āreṣ in Ezra 4:4 and Persian Imperial Administration." In *Judah and the Judeans in the Persian Period*, edited by Oded Lipschits, et al., 123-45. Winona Lake, IN: Eisenbrauns, 2006.

———. "Because of the Dread upon Them." In *The World of Achaemenid Persia: History, Art, and Society in Iran and the Ancient Near East: Proceedings of a Conference at the British Museum, 29th September-1st October, 2005*, edited by John Curtiset et al., 457-69. New York: Tauris, 2010.

———. "Did Second Temple High Priests Possess the *Urim* and *Thummim*?" *JHS* 7.3 (2007) 1-25. http://jhsonline.org/Articles/article_64.pdf.

———. *Ezra: A Commentary*. Critical Commentary. Sheffield: Sheffield Phoenix, 2015.

Galling, Kurt. "The Gōlā-List according to Ezra 2 and Nehemiah 7." *JBL* 70 (1951) 149-58.

Grabbe, Lester L. *Ezra-Nehemiah*. Old Testament Readings. Routledge: London, 1998.

Harrington, Hannah K. "Interpreting Leviticus in the Second Temple Period: Struggling with Ambiguity." In *Reading Leviticus: A Conversation with Mary Douglas*, edited by John F. A. Sawyer, 214-29. JSOTSup 227. Sheffield: Sheffield Academic, 1996.

Hjelm, Ingrid. *The Samaritans and Early Judaism: A Literary Analysis*. JSOTSup 303. Sheffield: Sheffield Academic, 2000.

Houtman, C. "The Urim and Thummim: A New Suggestion." *VT* 40 (1990) 229-32.

Japhet, Sara. "The Expulsion of The Foreign Women (Ezra 9-10): The Legal Basis, Precedents, and Consequences for the Definition of Jewish Identity." In *"Sieben Augen auf einem Stein" (Sach 3,9): Studien zur Literatur des Zweiten Tempels: Festschrift für Ina Willi-Plein zum 65. Geburtstag*, edited by Friedhelm Hartenstein and Michael Pietsch, 141-61. Neukirchen-Vluyn: Neukirchener, 2007.

———. "Law and 'The Law' in Ezra-Nehemiah." In *Proceedings of the 9th World Congress of Jewish Studies Panel Sessions: Biblical Studies and Ancient Near East*, 99-115. Jerusalem: Magnes, 1988.

———. "People and Land in the Restoration Period." In *Das Land Israel in biblischer Zeit: Jerusalem-Symposium 1981 der Hebräischen Universität und der Georg-August-Universität*. Göttinger theologische Arbeiten 25. Göttingen: Vandenhoeck & Ruprecht, 1983.

Johnson, Willa M. *The Holy Seed Has Been Defiled: The Interethnic Marriage Dilemma in Ezra 9-10*. Hebrew Bible Monographs 33. Sheffield: Sheffield Phoenix, 2011.

Klawans, Jonathan. *Impurity and Sin in Ancient Judaism*. Oxford: Oxford University Press, 2000.

Klein, Ralph W. *Ezra-Nehemiah*. New Interpeter's Bible 3. Nashville: Abingdon, 1999.

Knoppers, Gary N. "Ethnicity, Genealogy, Geography, and Change: The Judean Communities of Babylon and Jerusalem in the Story of Ezra." In *Community Identity in Judean Historiography: Biblical and Comparative Perspectives*, edited by Gary Knoppers, et al., 147-71. Winona Lake, IN: Eisenbrauns, 2009.

———. "Intermarriage, Social Complexity, and Ethnic Diversity in the Genealogy of Judah." *JBL* 120 (2001) 15-30.

Bibliography

———. *Jews and Samaritans: The Origins and History of Their Early Relations.* New York: Oxford University Press, 2013.

Knowles, Melody D. *Centrality Practiced: Jerusalem in the Religious Practice of Yehud and the Diaspora in the Persian Period.* Archaeology and Biblical Studies 16. Atlanta: SBL, 2006.

Lau, H.W. Peter. "Gentile Incorporation into Israel in Ezra–Nehemiah?" *Bib* 90 (2009) 356–73.

Maccoby, Hyam. "Holiness and Purity: The Holy People in Leviticus and Ezra–Nehemiah." In *Reading Leviticus: A Conversation with Mary Douglas*, edited by John F. A. Sawyer, 153–74. JSOTSup 227. Sheffield: Sheffield Academic, 1996.

Milgrom, Jacob. "The Concept of *Ma'al* in the Bible and the Ancient Near East." *JAOS* 96 (1976) 236–47.

Moffat, Donald P. "The Metaphor at Stake in Ezra 9:8." *VT* 63 (2013) 290–98. https://doi.org/10.1163/15685330-12341111.

Myers, Jacob M. *Ezra–Nehemiah*. Anchor Bible 14. New York: Double Day, 1965.

Na'aman, Nadav. "Saul, Benjamin and the Emergence of 'Biblical Israel' (Part 2)." *ZAW* 121 (2009) 335–49. https://doi.org/10.1515/ZAW.2009.023.

Oded, Bustenay. "The Time of Zerubbabel vis-à-vis the Time of Ezra: Between 'Holy People' and 'Holy Seed.'" In *Built by Wisdom, Established by Understanding: Essays on Biblical and Near Eastern Literature in Honor of Adele Berlin*, edited by Maxine L. Grossman, 241–66. Studies and Texts in Jewish History and Culture 23. Bethesda, MD: University Press of Maryland, 2013.

Olyan, Saul M. "Purity Ideology in Ezra–Nehemiah as a Tool to Reconstruct the Community." *JSJ* 35 (2004) 1–16.

Oswald, Wolfgang. "Foreign Marriages and Citizenship in Persian Period Judah." *JHS* 12 (2012) 1–17. https://doi.org/10.5508/jhs.2012.v12.a6.

Pakkala, Juha. "The Exile and the Exiles in the Ezra Tradition." In *Concept of Exile in Ancient Israel and Its Historical Contexts*, edited by Ehud Ben Zvi, et al., 91–102. BZAW 404. Berlin: de Gruyter, 2010.

Propp, William Henry. *Exodus 1–18*. Anchor Bible 2. New York: Doubleday, 1999.

Prosic, Tamara. *The Development and Symbolism of Passover until 70 CE*. JSOTSup 414. London: T. & T. Clark International, 2004.

Reddit, Paul L. *Ezra–Nehemiah*. Smyth & Helwys Commentary. Macon, GA: Smyth & Helwys, 2014.

Roberts, J. J. M. *First Isaiah: A Commentary*. Hermeneia. Minneapolis: Fortress, 2015.

Rom-Shiloni, Dalit. *Exclusive Inclusivity: Identity Conflicts between the Exiles and the People Who Remained (Sixth–Fifth Centuries BCE)*. LHBOTS 543. New York: Bloomsbury, 2013.

———. "From Ezekiel to Ezra–Nehemiah: Shifts of Group Identities within Babylonian Exilic Ideology." In *Judah and the Judeans in the Achaemenid Period: Negotiating Identity in an International Context,* edited by Oded Lipschits, et al., 127–54. Winona Lake, IN: Eisenbrauns, 2011.

Ron, Zvi. "The First Confrontation with the Samaritans (Ezra 4)." *JBQ* 43 (2015) 117–21.

Saysell, Csilla. *"According to the Law": Reading Ezra 9–10 as Christian Scripture*. Winona Lake, IN: Eisenbrauns, 2012.

Segal, J. B. *The Hebrew Passover: From the Earliest Times to AD 70*. London Oriental Series 12. London: Oxford University Press, 1963.

Bibliography

Shepherd, David J., and Christopher J. H. Wright. *Ezra and Nehemiah*. Two Horizons Old Testament Commentary. Grand Rapids: Eerdmans, 2018.

Smith-Christopher, Daniel L. "The Mixed Marriage Crisis in Ezra 9–10 and Nehemiah 13: A Study of the Sociology of Post-Exilic Judaean Community." In *Second Temple Studies 2: Temple Community in the Persian Period*, edited by Tamara C. Eskenazi and Kent H. Richards, 243–65. JSOTSup 175. Sheffield: Sheffield Academic, 1994.

Southwood, Katherine. *Ethnicity and the Mixed Marriage Crisis in Ezra 9–10: An Anthropological Approach*. Oxford; Oxford University Press, 2012.

———. "The Holy Seed: The Significance of Endogamous Boundaries and Their Transgression in Ezra 9–10." In *Judah and the Judeans in the Achaemenid Period: Negotiating Identity in an International Context*, edited by Oded Lipschits, 189–224. Winona Lake, IN: Eisenbrauns, 2011.

Talmon, Shemaryahu. "Ezra and Nehemiah." In *The Literary Guide to the Bible*, edited by Robert Alter, et al., 357–64. Cambridge: Harvard University Press, 1987.

Thames, John Tracy Jr. "A New Discussion of the Meaning of the Phrase *'am hāʾāreṣ* in the Hebrew Bible." *JBL* 130 (2011) 109–25.

Thiessen, Matthew. "The Function of a Conjunction: Inclusivist or Exclusivist Strategies in Ezra 6.19–21 and Nehemiah 10.29–30?" *JSOT* 34 (2009) 63–79.

Uspenskiĭ, Boris Andreevich. *A Poetics of Composition: The Structure of the Artistic Text and Typology of a Compositional Form*. Berkeley: University of California Press, 1983.

Watts, John D. W. *Isaiah 1–33*. Word Biblical Commentary 24. Waco, TX: Word, 1985.

Williamson, H. G. M. *Ezra, Nehemiah*. Word Biblical Commentary 16. Waco, TX: Word, 1985.

———. "The Family in Persian Period Judah: Some Textual Reflections." In *Symbiosis, Symbolism, and the Power of the Past: Canaan, Ancient Israel, and their Neighbors from the Late Bronze Age through Roman Palestina*, edited by William G. Dever and Seymour Gitin, 469–85. Winona Lake, IN: Eisenbrauns, 2003.

———. "Welcome Home." In *The Historian and the Bible: Essays in Honour of Lester L. Grabbe*, edited by Philip R. Davies, 113–23. LHBOTS 530. New York: Bloomsbury, 2010.

Wilton, Patrick. "More Cases of *Waw Explicativum*." *VT* 44 (1994) 125–28.

Yoo, Philip Young. *Ezra and the Second Wilderness*. Oxford: Oxford University Press, 2017.

Younger, K. Lawson, ed. *The Context of Scripture*. Vol. 4: *Supplements*. Leiden/Boston: Brill, 2017.

www.ingramcontent.com/pod-product-compliance
Lightning Source LLC
Chambersburg PA
CBHW071510150426
43191CB00009B/1473